D1453682

Voces

Voces

Latino Students on Life in the United States

Maria M. Carreira and Tom Beeman

 PRAEGER

AN IMPRINT OF ABC-CLIO, LLC
Santa Barbara, California • Denver, Colorado • Oxford, England

Library of Congress Cataloging-in-Publication Data

Carreira, Maria M.

Voces : Latino students on life in the United States / Maria M. Carreira and Tom Beeman.

pages cm

Includes index.

ISBN 978-1-4408-0351-2 (hard copy : alk. paper) — ISBN 978-1-4408-0352-9 (ebook)   1. Hispanic American youth—Attitudes.   2. Hispanic American youth—Ethnic identity.   3. Hispanic American youth—Social conditions. 4. United States—Ethnic relations.   I. Beeman, Tom.   II. Title.

E184.S75C38   2014

305.235089'968073—dc23   2014024805

ISBN: 978-1-4408-0351-2

EISBN: 978-1-4408-0352-9

18   17   16   15   14   1   2   3   4   5

This book is also available on the World Wide Web as an eBook.
Visit www.abc-clio.com for details.

Praeger
An Imprint of ABC-CLIO, LLC

ABC-CLIO, LLC
130 Cremona Drive, P.O. Box 1911
Santa Barbara, California 93116-1911

This book is printed on acid-free paper ∞

Manufactured in the United States of America

Contents

Preface vii

ONE: *Voces* from School 1

TWO: *Voces* about Language 39

THREE: *Voces* about Culture 79

FOUR: *Voces* about Family 117

FIVE: Family Life, Latino-American Style 155

Afterword 175

Index 179

Preface

Hispanics are the nation's largest minority group, making up more than 50 million people, or about 16.5% of the U.S. population. Among the 30 million young people ages 18 to 24, 6 million, or 20%, are Hispanics. . . . As students in nursery school progress through kindergarten and into elementary school and high school, Hispanic students will make up a rising share of public high school students and all public school students in coming years. According to the U.S. Census Bureau, by 2036 Hispanics are projected to compose one-third of the nation's children ages 3 to 17.[1]

These words from the Pew Research Center's Hispanic Trends Project leave no doubt that our nation's destiny is inextricably linked to that of Latino youth. In effect, our future is only as bright and promising as that of its largest minority population.

And what does the future of Latino youth look like?

A number of indicators paint a distressing picture of Latino youth, from high dropout and teen pregnancy rates to low test scores and college participation rates. However, these indicators alone do not provide a complete likeness of this population, and to the central premise of this book, they do not capture its promise. To grasp that promise, it is essential to listen to Latino youth. Their stories speak to the personal strengths and cultural resources that prove fundamental in defying the odds and achieving success.

How did they come to possess these strengths, and how can other students develop them too?

The hundreds of comments and anecdotes in this book speak to these issues, as they provide a picture of Latino youth that goes beyond the mere listing of performance indicators or the discussion of the problems that assail them. The collective voices of the youth featured here echo the conclusions that "the pathway to success for Latino youth requires a motivation to succeed, a plan of action, a willingness and need to act on one's intentions, and perhaps most importantly, a support system of family, friends, teachers, and community to help them reach toward their goals."[2] These voices also speak to the formidable power of *resilience*—the capacity to tap into personal, cultural, and social tools and resources for maintaining well-being and finding meaning under difficult situations.

The majority of the comments and anecdotes were collected over the course of many years teaching Latino youth at the college level. Pseudonyms have been used to protect the privacy of our students. What started out as a simple class assignment for our students turned into this project as it became evident to us that these stories are interesting, inspiring, and vitally important to understanding the ingredients of Latino success. In our view, one of the most important insights to emerge from this exercise is that many of the solutions to the problems that assail Latino youth reside within Latino youth themselves, as well as their families and communities. More broadly, these stories underscore the value of universal, time-honored principles and practices that are conducive to the well-being and success of all youth, including love and respect of family, sense of duty, and sense of purpose.

We approached this project from the position of "humble experts," a technique used by psychologists to avoid stereotyping, which involves showing respectful curiosity and adopting a humble not-knowing attitude. In keeping with this approach, we asked our students to relate a key childhood experience and comment on its larger significance. We also asked them to share with us what they would want teachers, school administrators, and other people in positions of leadership to know about U.S. Latinos. Other Latinos, besides our students, have also contributed to this book—neighbors, friends, and strangers we met on the Internet, all of whom were generous enough to let us feature their stories. We are deeply grateful to all.

Insights for these Latino youths fall into four general topics: schooling, language, culture, and family life, each of which constitutes the focus of a separate chapter. Together, these chapters address what started out as the driving question behind this book: what is it like to grow up Latino in the United States? In addition—and arguably more importantly—these chapters address a second set of questions that emerged over the course of writing this book: what are the pathways to academic achievement and social well-being forged by Latino youth? And, how can we, as a society, exploit these pathways to tackle the problems faced by this population and derive benefit from their strengths?

Chapter 1 presents the leading factors behind the so-called Latino academic gap from the perspective of the learners. Chapter 2 examines the rewards and challenges of bilingualism and explores how issues of language permeate all spheres of life, from school and home to peer interactions. Chapter 3 traces the complex interplay of cultural and social factors at play in the development of Latino children: issues such as identity, race, culture, and perceptions by others. Chapter 4 focuses on family life, in particular, how children navigate the pressures of balancing generational, cultural, and linguistic differences. Chapter 5 differs from the others in that rather than focusing on a particular topic, it features three very different Latino families following what turn out to be very similar pathways to achieving the American dream. Our goals for this final chapter are threefold: one, to convey a sense of the range of experiences that characterize Latino immigration; two, to capture the family resources available to Latino youth in action and interaction over the course of time; and three, to weave together the themes of the previous chapters, by way of conclusion. Altogether, these chapters paint a fuller picture of Latino youth than that conveyed by labels such as "underprivileged" or "at risk," which are so frequently applied to this population. Without denying the harsh realities associated with such labels, that picture brings into focus other labels that apply to this population as well, including resourceful, resilient, and promising. That picture is also a call to action, beckoning and challenging us to follow the pathways to well-being forged by Latino youth.

Throughout this book, the personal and autobiographical is presented against the backdrop of the academic research. In so doing, we aim to make this material accessible to a general reader seeking a practical understanding of the subject matter, as well as a professional reader, such as a teacher or school administrator, looking for a deeper understanding of the issues. We have also strived to make the book suitable for use in academic settings. Accordingly, each chapter closes with a list of resources and thought-provoking questions, which can serve as the basis for collegial discussions or class assignments.

In keeping with the focus on this book, a word about our own stories is in order. Maria was born in Cuba and immigrated to the United States at age 11, and Tom is originally from Cleveland, Ohio, and has been living in Southern California since he was a young child. In a sense, this project was born over 15 years ago when Tom was a student of Maria at California State University, Long Beach, where she is a professor of Spanish linguistics. Today, Tom is a high school Spanish teacher as well as a former university administrator and TESOL teacher trainer. What started out as a mentoring relationship developed into a deep friendship and a productive professional partnership.

This project, however, is more than the combined sum of our efforts. Special recognition is due to our editor, Kim Kennedy-White, who so patiently put up with delays, gently but firmly nudged us along, and greatly improved our manuscript with her suggestions. Family and friends have also been indispensable. Their presence bears out a central premise of this book, namely, that there is no greater resource than the support and encouragement of loved ones. This book is dedicated to them, in particular, at Maria's end, to her immigrant grandfathers, Domingo Carreira Vilariño (Abuelo Pan) and Manuel Morán Gutiérrez, who opened doors to wondrous new worlds for their children and grandchildren, to her parents, Domingo Carreira Pérez and Marta Morán Arco, who embody the best of Latino parenting; to her husband, Bartlett Mel, who has shared the best of American culture with her and has so enthusiastically embraced the best of Cuban culture, to their children Gabriel, Francis, Margot, and Carmen, who will write the next chapter in her family's immigration story, to her teachers, particularly those at Saint Scholastica High School, who practiced *additive schooling* years ahead of their time, and to her friends Ana Roca, Najib Redouane, Olga Kagan, Claire Chik, and the Pascucci family, whose own immigration stories are a source of inspiration and awe. For his part, Tom Beeman would like to dedicate this book to his high school Spanish teacher Yolanda Swenson. It's because of her passion for teaching that he decided to become a Spanish teacher himself. Her guidance and support can only be expressed through her favorite saying, *¡Hay chinelas de huangochis!*. Originally used by her grandmother as an expression of disappointment, in the hands of this gifted teacher this phrase became a good-natured but firm call to her students to do their best. He would also like to thank his fellow parishioners at St. John of God Catholic Church in Norwalk, California, for all of their insight and time to help contribute to this book, and to Alex Evanovich for her encouragement and guidance through the actual writing process.

As educators, we are humbled and heartened by the courage, wisdom, and resiliency of our students. Their stories and insights merit attention not just for what they reveal about growing up Latino in the United States but also for the deeper human lessons they offer—lessons about grace, tenacity, and resourcefulness under duress. It is our hope that our readers—be they professionals who deal with Latinos in the course of their work or simply individuals who are curious about this vital population of Americans—will be inspired to view and interact with Latinos from a new perspective.

NOTES

1. Richard Fry and Mark Hugo Lopez, "Hispanic Student Enrollments Reach New Highs in 2011." *Pew Hispanic Center*, August 20, 2012. http://www.pewhispanic.org/2012/08/20/ii-hispanic-public-school-enrollments/.

2. Alberto Cabrera, "Pathways for Latino Youth." WCER Research Highlights 16, no. 4 (Winter 2004–Winter 2005). http://www.wcer.wisc.edu/publications/highlights/v16n4.pdf.

ONE

Voces from School

THE LATINO EDUCATIONAL EXPERIENCE: WHY IT MATTERS TO EVERYONE

What is it like to grow up Latino in the United States? This is the over-arching question behind this book.

To answer this question, each chapter focuses on a different component of the experience of U.S. Latinos, from schooling to language, culture, and family life. Together, the chapters paint a picture of this experience.

To grasp the significance of this question and appreciate why we have chosen to open this book with the topic of schooling, it is essential to widen our field of vision from Latinos to U.S. society at large.

A study by the *Pew Hispanic Center* notes:

Latinos' success at entering and graduating from college affects not only their wellbeing but also the nation's wellbeing. Between 2000 and 2025 the white working age population will decline by five million as baby boomers retire from the labor force. Working age Latinos are projected to increase by 18 million. Thus, the vitality of the U.S. work force increasingly depends on Hispanic educational progress.[1]

If, as the phrase goes, demography is destiny, then the future of America is inextricably bound to that of Latino children. Nearly one out of every five children (23%) in American schools is Latino. This number is significantly higher in some of this nation's largest public school systems, including San Antonio, Texas (87%), Los Angeles, California (71%), Miami, Florida (56%), and Houston, Texas (55%). In California, the nation's most populous state, Latino children make up 50 percent of the public school population.[2]

These numbers add up to an inescapable conclusion: America cannot afford to leave Latino children behind. Ensuring their success in school and ultimately their full participation in the workforce of the 21st century is a priority of the highest importance. With this in mind, this chapter explores the school experiences of these children, as relayed by them and documented in the research literature. Reflecting on the student comments in this chapter, it is hard not to notice how remarkably insightful Latino children are in describing the causes behind the so-called Latino achievement gap. Their insightful comments attest to their perceptiveness, level of engagement, and aptitude for learning, as they also point to the failure of the educational system to exploit these strengths.

LATINO SCHOOLING BY THE NUMBERS

Demographics

46: Percentage of Latinos who attend elementary school in a high poverty area (*vs.* 4% Asian/Pacific Islander, 14% of whites, and 34% of blacks)[3]

45: Percentage of young Latinos who are enrolled in college (*vs.* 45% of young blacks, 51% of young whites, 67% of young Asians)[4]

24.7: Percentage of elementary school students in the United States who are Latino[5]

21: Percentage of high school students in the United States who are Latino[6]

20: Percentage of immigrant Latino students who live with someone other than a parent or grandparent (*vs.* 3% of nonimmigrant Latino students)[7]

16.5: Percentage of college students who are Hispanic[8]

7: Percentage of public school teachers who are Latino[9]

Attitudes

94: Percentage of Latinos who consider education to be extremely important or very important[10]

63: Percentage of Latinos who give their local school a grade of A or B[11]

89: Percentage of Latinos over 16 who consider a college education to be necessary to getting ahead (*vs.* 74% of the general population)[12]

84: Percentage of the Latino population who consider discrimination to be a problem in schools[13]

75: Percentage of Latinos who say that discrimination is a problem in school[14]

70: Percentage of Latino students who speak a language other than English at home[15]

77: Percentage of Latinos youth who say their parents think going to college is more important than getting a job after high school[16]

48: Percentage of Latino youth who expect to get a college degree (*vs.* 60% of the general population)[17]

44: Percentage of Latino youth who believe that cultural issues are a major reason why Latino youth do not perform as well in school[18]

Performance

76: Percentage of Latinos who are high school graduates (*vs.* 90% Asians, 88% of whites, and 81% black)[19]

13: Percentage of young Latinos who have a bachelor's degree (*vs.* 53% of young Asians, 39% of young whites, and 19% of blacks)[20]

THE STATE OF LATINOS' EDUCATIONAL ATTAINMENT

Leading academic indicators paint a distressing picture of Latino students. According to the National Assessment of Educational Progress (i.e., The Nation's Report Card), one out of every three Latinos in grades K-12 is performing below grade level in reading and math. At 14 percent, Latino high school dropout rates are the highest in the nation, notably higher than those of white students (5%) and African American students (7%).[21] Foreign-born Latinos are particularly at risk, being nearly three times as likely to drop out (28%) than those born in this country (9%).[22] Teen mothers are also very vulnerable. In a survey of female dropouts, almost one half said that becoming a parent played a role in their decision to leave school, and one-third said it was a major factor.[23]

The consequences of higher dropout rates are serious and far-reaching, affecting not just individuals but also society at large. They include higher rates of unemployment, higher reliance on public assistance and increased health problems, higher criminal behavior, and higher rates of incarceration.[24] Speaking to these and other realities, Patricia Gándara of the Civil Rights Project/*Proyecto Derechos Civiles* writes: "The most urgent problem for the American Education system has a Latino face."[25]

While we agree with the earlier assessment, we would add that the greatest potential for the American education system also has a Latino face. With firsthand knowledge of the problems that assail this system, they are our go-to experts on the fixes. Bilingual and bicultural, they have much to contribute to the workforce in today's global economy. But with all the negatives surrounding these students, is it realistic to think that this potential can ever be realized? Professor Eugene García, dean of Arizona State University's College of Education and one of the nation's authorities on Latino children, believes it is provided enough resources are brought to bear on this situation. He writes:

> If the treatment of Hispanics in our educational institutions is like the seismic indicators of an impending earthquake, a set of indicators that are now sending signals of coming dangers, then how we react to those signals is important. We can ignore these, but the dangers will not go away. We can respond to them minimally, study them some more, and prepare for the worst. Or we can marshal the intellectual resources in ways that will make the inevitable an opportunity from which we can benefit.[26]

Giving rise to hope, some indicators of educational attainment for Latinos are trending positive. Most notably, the number of Latino youth who have completed high school and are attending college is at an all-time high.[27] Studies show that improvements such as these can have strong and far-reaching ripple effects in society. For example, in California, where the ratio of high school graduates to dropouts is three to one, it is estimated that if dropout rates were cut by half, the murders and aggravated assaults would be sharply reduced and the state's economy would be stimulated by an additional $12 billion.[28] Focusing on minority graduation rates in the nation as a whole, the Alliance for Excellent Education estimates that "if the nation's high schools and colleges raise the graduation rates of Hispanic, African-American, and Native-American students to the levels of White students by 2020, the potential increase in personal income across the nation would add, conservatively, more than $310 billion to the U.S. economy."[29]

The student narratives provide a blueprint for achieving these and other outcomes. In particular, they point to the importance of (1) grappling with the obstacles and deficiencies in the area of education that are holding Latinos back, and (2) tapping underdeveloped resources to create opportunities for these students and, ultimately, society. We turn to the first of these points next, leaving the second point to the end of this chapter.

WHAT'S HOLDING LATINOS BACK?

The issues behind the Latino achievement gap are varied and complex, involving linguistic, socioeconomic, cultural, and structural factors, and affecting children differently, depending on their circumstances and personal characteristics. Given the complexity of this situation, our goal for this chapter is not to provide a comprehensive overview of the issues or even an in-depth analysis of a few. Rather, our focus is on the issues identified by our students as most impactful. Taken individually, as they are presented in the sections that follow, these issues are alarming enough. Taken together, they add up to a devastating picture of an academically impoverished and emotionally bruising school environment.

The first accounts featured in this chapter spotlight many of the issues that occupy us, from deficiencies in the teaching of English and, more generally, the education of Spanish-speaking children to the sense of isolation and marginalization felt by these children in a school environment that is not always welcoming to them. What makes these accounts particularly valuable, and a fitting place to start this discussion, is that they paint a picture of the combined effects of these issues on the academic, social, and psychological development of Latino children. In so doing, they speak to what expert Angela Valenzuela calls "subtractive schooling," a situation whereby schools rob students of the resources associated with their home culture and erode their relationships in school.[30]

Strong and resourceful, the young women in these first accounts managed to rise above their circumstances. The resources and pathways that proved valuable to them, along with other strategies used by Latino youth, are examined at the end of this chapter.

The first account in this chapter is by Ana Colucci (not her real name). A successful and confident student in her native Argentina, Ana's self-concept was shaken when her family moved to California. In this essay, she relays the obstacles she encountered in her first months in an American school and how with patience, talent, hard work, and the support of her parents, she learned English and claimed back her status as an excellent student. Today, Colucci is a successful veterinarian in Southern California. She appears once again at the end of this book, in Chapter 5, along with the members of her family.

When I came to the United States, I knew things would be different. I was 11 and going into the 6th grade. I only knew the basics in English, so my parents and I decided I would go to the 5th grade for a couple of months in order to get the feel for the classes and also listen to some English. I had always loved school in Argentina and always did well, so I was not concerned; I was glad I was starting in a stress free environment instead of being thrown into it. My teacher seemed nice the first day when the principal brought me to the class. I picked a seat in the back and began to soak in all the noise that would hopefully soon make sense. Everything was going well until one day the teacher hands me a piece of paper with a huge red F and started talking to me loudly, almost yelling, that I hadn't been doing my homework. She embarrassed me in front of the whole class, especially since I didn't know how to respond. I wanted to cry. The teacher had obviously not understood the situation. . . . I was supposed to be an observer and not be graded for work because I had already completed 5th grade in Argentina. I wanted to tell her, explain the facts to her, but I couldn't express myself.

Being faced with the possibility of a bad grade was a huge self-esteem blow. I started faking being sick and crying every day to try to avoid going to school. I am thankful for other rewarding learning experiences in later years for helping me stay focused in school and love learning again. The inability to react to the teacher's comments also put me in a constant state of anxiousness. I was worried that she might say something to me again and I felt powerless for not being able to respond and defend myself. Lack of communication was a big problem; between my family and the principal, the principal and the teacher, the teacher and me. . . . Something along the way had gone wrong. Going to school was supposed to be a stress free way to get accustomed to how things happen in this country and make some friends. It had turned into my first taste of failure. After my parents talked to the school again, they arranged for a fellow student to help me and translate during class. This student, however, was not the best friend a new student should have. He was a troublemaker, spoke back to the teacher all the time, and was known to be a bit of a bully. I'm sure he didn't like the idea of being forced to translate for the foreign kid. I still doubt if he even told me the right information, because I could tell he was making fun of me. I am not stupid; I just didn't know English.

More culture barriers made themselves evident later that week. On Friday it was a special day when we got a break and played games. The game of the week was baseball. I had never heard nor seen this game . . . and I can say it is the hardest thing to try to learn by watching. Needless to say it provided another embarrassing, awkward opportunity for me: another thing to make me stand out in front of my classmates, another thing for me to fail at, another thing for me to hate about school, another thing for people to make fun of me, another obvious indication of how out of place I was in this country; I couldn't even play a fun game correctly. Nobody realized that in most of the world, baseball is not a major sport, and that perhaps I wouldn't know how to play. The teacher did not let me sit the game out; apparently even fun time was a requirement and I had to do more than just observe. Nobody decided to teach me once I gestured that I didn't know what to do when they handed me the bat. I cowardly walked to the plate, hit the ball and ran to first base, as I had seen my colleagues do. There I stopped . . . I was supposed to run again, I guess, I don't even remember, because I was again fighting back the tears. Being a public failure was not something I was accustomed to. In Argentina, I was a good student and a decent athlete, but that didn't matter in the new country, I was out of my element. Baseball became a symbol of everything that was different in this country, everything that I didn't understand.

I survived those 2 months of "observing" in elementary school and moved on to middle school. Oddly enough, it was better than I expected. I learned much of my American English from summer school and watching countless hours of television (thanks in part to Full House and Family Matters). When 6th grade came around, I was ready. I was placed in ESL class (English as a Second Language) but the teacher realized my English level was beyond ESL stage and she asked me to leave. However, the regular English class was full so I fell through the cracks. There was no place for me. I was in an English language no-mans land, too good for ESL and too late to enroll in English class. Along with two other students in the same situation (a Brazilian and another Argentine whom I befriended) we were put in charge of watering the "secret garden" the English class had planted after reading the book by the same name instead of having English class. When the weather was not agreeable for watering, we sat in the "library," which was a trailer with a few books and tables to work on.

In 6th grade, I was able to make friends, do well in school and choose not to play baseball at recess and play soccer instead. The rest is history. I consider myself a strong person with a great support group, my family. I was lucky because I didn't experience any outstanding hardships or discrimination; I was able to overcome my first negative experience and try to adjust. Now, I even understand baseball, although I still don't play it. It takes a lot of hard work and perseverance because people are not always willing to help, and those who are willing don't always know how to help.

A native of El Salvador, Isbelda Sánchez also experienced difficulties upon arriving in the United States at the age of seven. Unlike Ana, who always had college aspirations, it took a special program in high school to convince Isbelda that she was college material. A recent college graduate with a degree in Spanish translation and interpretation, Isbelda works for a Japanese company in Southern California, handling interactions with clients in Latin America.

Starting school with no friends and no way of communicating was very hard. I still remember coming home crying because I did not like school. Since the first day of the first grade up until the 6th life seemed to be always harder for me than for other students.

I remember going to elementary school and feeling out of place and alienated from everyone. I would be sent to sit in a bench with other kids that did not speak any English. The teacher aid would come and review the alphabet with us and teach us phonics. During recess I would be alone without friends. My cousin was in the same school, but instead of helping me she would make fun of me and tell me I was a loser. I would always be isolated because I did not speak English. When I got my first report card, I had many D's and F's.

There were days when I would beg my mom to not take me to school. I would even pretend to be sick because I detested school. At one point I wasn't sure I was going to make it to high school, let alone college. I was determined however to pass my classes.

When I started high school, I was placed in a class named AVID (Advancement Via Individual Determination). This was the best thing that ever happened to me in school. AVID is a program that helps students get to a four-year college. When I started high school, I really did not think that I would ever graduate or go to college. However, AVID gave me so much hope that eventually I became a better student. One of the most important things it did was to help me feel like I wasn't just a "Spanish-speaker," I was also a part of a group, a school family, as well as an individual with my own needs and ways of being.

My journey through school has not been an easy one. I have felt like an outcast many times just because of my English. But I will make it.

The issues described by Ana and Isbelda are examined one by one in the sections that follow.

BEING JUST A SPANISH SPEAKER: LINGUISTIC PROFILING AND THE ESL TRACK

This section derives its title from the juxtaposition of two ideas in Isbelda's essay, namely, the idea of becoming a better student and that of being viewed as more than just a Spanish speaker. As we explain in this section, viewing Latino children exclusively through the prism of Spanish leads to linguistic profiling, with negative consequences. This point will be revisited in Chapter 5, in the context of discussing seemingly contradictory viewpoints expressed by youth surrounding the treatment of Spanish in school.

Many Latino children either speak English at home or learn it soon after starting school.[31] Despite this, all too many are placed in ESL (English as a Second Language), also known as English Language Learner (ELL), classes, on the basis that they indicate on the school's home language survey that they speak Spanish at home. The following students reflect on this practice:

1. My siblings and I were all born here, yet because we have Mexican parents, they (the schools) believe we can't speak English fluently. The reason for this is because when our parents are supposed to enroll us in Kindergarten, the school asks which language is spoken at home and if they choose Spanish, they treat us differently. Even though we were able to speak better English than Spanish, in middle school they put us in bilingual classes because of what our parents wrote when we were only five years old. The district puts students in those classes because they receive more money for those that are in any ELL class.

2. I did not have a heavy accent like others in my elementary school. I went through elementary school without any difficulties but I remember having to take an ESL exam to be labeled a non-ESL student, which was very confusing to me because I was always in an all-English class except for one semester in Kindergarten that I was in an all-Spanish class. Later I found out that students are usually labeled ESL because their parents put on the school application that the language spoken at home is Spanish and the school system sees that as being ESL.

3. One thing I really didn't like about being perceived as a Spanish-speaker was that when I was in elementary school, about fourth or fifth

grade, my teachers began to assume that just because I was a Spanish-speaker I wouldn't do well in English. They would put me in the basic type of English classes. But I soon advanced because they figured out that the classes they put me in were too easy for me. Now that I am older, English is the subject I'm best at and I'm still speaking Spanish at home.

Placement in the ESL track has profound consequences for Latino students, regardless of whether it's warranted or not. As discussed below, seemingly innocuous practices and perspectives associated with ESL can actually take away from the schooling experience of Latino students, separating them from their peers, subjecting them to undue scrutiny, and eroding their self-esteem.

1. I was not happy being in ESL because not all of my friends were in the program. I remember when I was in my second grade class, my teacher was going over a fun activity and I had to go with ESL when at that time I wished I did not have to go. ESL made me feel different, not unique, but sort of like an outcast to all the other regular students. I wanted to get out of the program as soon as possible, so I worked very hard.

2. When I started school I only knew how to speak Spanish. I entered elementary school and they classified me as an ESL student. In first grade, my teacher taught me to read and write in English and Spanish. I was in ESL classes until 5th grade. I didn't understand why I had to take ESL exams every year after I left elementary school. When I entered high school my AVID (Advancement Via Individual Determination) teacher gave me the opportunity to enroll in honors English classes. I was very proud of myself because I felt that I had finally left behind the ESL label. One way, during my sophomore year I was in my English class, with people I considered very intelligent. A man came and he asked my teacher if I and another student would be able to leave the class to take an ESL exam! I almost died of embarrassment because the people in my class must have assumed that I didn't know as much as they thought. I left class and went to a special room to take the exam. They asked me stupid questions, like if I knew how to say "broom" in English. I was angry and offended. I told this to my teacher and she tried to console me. She said that this would be the last year they would classify me as an ESL student. However, this classification continues to torment me now that I'm in college. Because I'm bilingual, many professors think that I don't know how to express myself in English well. An English professor

that I had in my second semester in college used the term "bilingual" as if it were the worst thing that could have happened in my life. He would look at my essays and he would always criticize me, stating that my problems with grammar and spelling were because I speak Spanish at home. He told me this so many times that I came to believe it.

3. Growing up, I learned English and Spanish. However, in elementary school when the teachers found out I was fluent in Spanish they automatically wanted to place me in "bilingual classes." These were really ESL classes for students who couldn't do regular work in English. I remember my mom being a bit upset by this—not because I didn't need the class—but because she felt it was unfair to students who actually needed this class. I was upset because I felt like I was less intelligent and could not participate and be as productive as the non-Latinos.

4. I always thought that being in ESL was something for students with a learning disability.

Where does this association between ESL and low intelligence and productivity come from? The negative academic outcomes associated with ESL have a lot to do with it.

For many students, the ESL track often acts as a gatekeeper, preventing them from taking challenging coursework, such as college preparatory, honors, and Advanced Placement (AP) courses, and forcing them into special Limited English Proficient (LEP) courses in the core areas of the curriculum (e.g., math, social studies, and science). Often, the language and coverage of material in such courses are not up to the academic standards of mainstream classes, leaving students unable to transition to mainstream (non-LEP) courses and rendering college out of reach. Compounding matters, states often require students to take an annual exam to demonstrate their proficiency in English as the only means of transitioning out of the ESL track, an exam that most native English speakers of similar age would not be able to pass.

Linked to this issue is the fact that the overwhelming majority of LEP students (85% according to one study) are actually conversant in everyday English but lack grade-level reading and writing skills.[32] To develop these skills, they need access to texts that are conceptually and linguistically challenging and that expose them to academic English, a formal version of English that uses advanced vocabulary, grammatical structures, phraseology, and rhetorical devices. Such materials, however, are in short supply in LEP courses.[33]

In the textbox, the schedules of three Californian LEP students in their junior and senior years of high school offer as compelling a picture as any of the academically impoverished schooling experience of large numbers of Latino youth. Deficient in core areas of the curriculum and lacking academic rigor, these programs of study fall short of giving students the skills they need for college, let alone to compete in today's world.[34]

STUDENT SCHEDULE

Saul (two years in the United States, attended ninth grade in Mexico, where he was in a college preparatory curriculum and took advanced mathematics courses) Sophomore year (2001)

Period 1: No class
Period 2: Language Development 1
Period 3: Language Development 2
Period 4: Native Spanish 1
Period 5: U.S. History (in Spanish)
Period 6: Math A (general, low level)
Period 7: Weightlifting

(Two courses meet college preparatory requirements: Spanish and U.S. History. No science is provided.)

Jose Luis (one year in the United States. Uneven academic history prior to immigration) Sophomore (2001)

Period 1: No class
Period 2: Language Development 1
Period 3: Language Development 1
Period 4: General Math (in English)
Period 5: Native Spanish 1
Period 6: Drawing 1
Period 7: No class

(One class prepares the student for college requirements: Spanish. No science or social science offered. Student failed English only math because he could not understand the teacher.)

Marisela (Long-term EL student, enrolled in California schools prior to entering high school) Senior year (2002)

Period 1: Power English
Period 2: Weight training
Period 3: ELD 5C
Period 4: Business Math
Period 5: Consumer Foods
Period 6: Floral Design

(None of the student's courses meets college preparatory criteria. The student took no laboratory science or math beyond Algebra 1, which she failed and received no credit.)

The narratives that follow shine a light on institutional practices and perspectives that further erode the learning experience of ESL students. As explained in the first comment, the practice of pulling students out of regular classes to teach them English has the effect of depriving them of instruction in the content areas. Using other students as translators—another common practice of schools—does not solve the problem because children do not generally have the skills and background to properly translate, let alone instruct their peers on subject knowledge. Bilingual teachers, on the other hand, do have such skills, but they are in short supply in gifted classes. As is the case in the second comment, ESL students who enroll in those classes are likely to struggle and risk failure, due to inadequate support. This type of binary thinking whereby ESL—and by logical extension, Spanish-speaker—is seen as being in opposition to gifted is at the heart of subtractive schooling.[35]

1. When I was in elementary school, I didn't know how to speak English and I was always confused by the materials used to review. When I was in second grade I was assigned a bilingual student who would translate everything for me. Personally, I don't think this was of any help because I didn't have to put forth any effort to understand the material because everything was explained to me. It wasn't until third grade that I was placed in a special program to begin to learn English. This was not a good idea because they took us out of our different classes to attend this special class and we were missing out on the subjects being taught in our regular classes keeping us down and causing many of us to repeat the year. I believe this caused problems for many students and it didn't motivate them to continue learning the language.

2. When it came time to move, my parents registered me in a new school, but every day I went to school it was a nightmare for me. When my parents enrolled me in the new school, they wanted me to be placed in bilingual classes but the principal commented that this wasn't possible because there were no bilingual teachers in the gifted program. My parents had two options: to let me be in the gifted class in which only English would be spoken, or to go to ESL classes for less successful children. My parents believed that I was better off in the gifted class because I should have learned to write and read in English in my bilingual classes at my old school. This transition affected me because my teachers never took the actual time to teach me English. This class impacted me a lot because I was used to always having the best grades in my classes, now I had the lowest scores in this new English class. This experienced caused me to lose a semester in the 4th grade because I didn't attend school because I didn't understand anything. Our governor needs to hire more bilingual teachers in our communities and place them in high levels like magnet or gifted programs, not only ESL.

ACADEMIC PROFILING

Many of the problems associated with the ESL track relate to the larger issue of academic profiling, which ultimately leads to disparate outcomes for Latino students. Practices associated with academic profiling include placement in less rigorous courses and messages that convey lower academic expectations and perpetuate cultural stereotypes. The emotional pain and academic harm inflicted by this state of affairs is plain in the following comments:

1. In elementary school I was on the honor roll and did well enough to receive acceptance to Coast Side School, a college prep public school serving grades 7th–12th. In grades 7th to 9th you must maintain a 2.5 GPA to stay enrolled and a 3.0 GPA during grades 10–12th. My mom wanted me to attend this school, but my teacher felt that I was unprepared for its rigorous curriculum. On the last day of 6th grade, my teacher pulled me aside with another student who was also going to Coast Side School. She told the other student that he would do just fine and she turned to me and proceeded to tell me that I was going to struggle and flunk out of Coast Side because of my poor writing skills. She then told me that I was accepted only because they had a diversity quota. I was crushed and immediately began to think that I

did not deserve to go to Coast Side. I graduated from Coast Side four years ago, but my teacher's comments have always stayed with me. All through high school, I felt I did not belong. It was particularly ironic to say that I would struggle with my writing because I always did well in language-based classes. I did struggle in math and science classes but never flunked out of school. Coast Side is predominately an Asian-American school with very few Latinos. That, in combination with my teacher's comments, made me feel out of place.

2. I have noticed that in some schools where there are many Latinos, there aren't special programs to prepare students for college. I think in part this is because there's a belief among teachers that there is no need for these programs because Latinos aren't interested in them or stand to benefit from them. . . . I remember an experience that I had with a counselor who, fortunately, is not at my old school any more. I was in 11th grade and I realized that it was time to get ready for college. I filled out a form to meet with a counselor. After several months, this lady called me to make an appointment. I found myself talking to a woman who barely said "hello" to me and showed very little interest in me. When I told her about my plans to go to college she looked at me as if thinking I was crazy. She gave me an application for the local community college and told me that this would be better for me because it was easier. This made me feel very disheartened.

3. Throughout my education I have noticed discrepancies in the treatment of others and myself. I grew up in the magnet programs of [a local school district] so I saw how the magnet kids got more funding and special treatment. The magnet programs offered me ample opportunity to succeed in life, but I couldn't help but feel guilty that I was one of very few Latinos benefiting from these programs (I was one of four Latinos in my school). At the beginning of every year, when the teachers saw my test scores, they almost always made me re-take the tests—I guess to make sure that I had not cheated. As the years passed, my anger grew because I was frustrated that my abilities were always seen as a fluke: I had to be cheating, I couldn't possibly be smart or hardworking. Because I was so young, I would just get angry. I had no understanding of the bigger picture. With time, I came to realize why this was happening. I was Latino, a woman, and my parents were poor—three major strikes.

4. In elementary school I remember taking placement exams. It appeared to me all the "brown kids" were all placed in the lower tracks. The worse

part about it was that the kids in the higher tracks were aware of what was going on. I remember feeling like we were second-class citizens— ignored, forced to use lower quality materials, and taught by assistants, not the teachers. I strongly believe that this planted the seed in me of "decremented deprivation," which followed me through my adolescent years. It wasn't until my brother started taking Chicano Latino courses in college and he shared his pride in our history that I feel competent enough to continue my education. Once I began taking these courses, I heard similar stories from other Latino students like me.

Academic profiling also helps explain the overrepresentation of language minority children in special education courses. At the elementary level, they are one-and-a-half times more likely than other students to be diagnosed as having a speech impairment or a learning disability, and at the high school level, they are twice as likely to be diagnosed as such.[36]

Why does this happen? One reason is that many teachers, administrators, and school staff who work with language minority children lack adequate training in areas such as bilingualism and language acquisition. As a result, they misconstrue normal patterns of development in bilingual children as being indicative of a disability.

A classic study of linguistic hallucination underscores the importance of proper training for teachers and tells a cautionary tale for educators called to make placement decisions involving language minority children. The subjects of the study, who were white student teachers, viewed three slightly different versions of a video, one with a white child, another with an African American child, and a third with a Mexican American child. Although all three versions had exactly the same audio—the voice of a child speaking standard English—they yielded tellingly different outcomes: student teachers consistently rated the Mexican American and African American children as more nonstandard in their use of language than the white child.[37]

A CLIMATE OF NEGLECT, INSENSITIVITY, AND HOSTILITY

Arguably, the biggest contributor to subtractive schooling is the climate of neglect, insensitivity, and, in some cases, outright hostility surrounding Latinos that permeates some schools. The anecdotes in this section speak to what it is like to attend school under the strain of that climate.

Internalizing the negative cultural stereotypes transmitted to them by their teachers and peers, the following students report feeling ashamed of their background and disconnected from school.

1. The schooling system does not relate to the Latino experience. It is Eurocentric and ignores minority issues. It's like we don't exist. They don't see us. The Latino community is the largest community in California but you wouldn't know it judging by what gets taught in school. This negligence angers me.

2. It was in middle school when I noticed that "los mexicanos" were sometimes outcasts. I had never noticed discrimination before that, but many of my friends didn't even know I was Mexican. Most of the Latinos were in remedial programs and just a few were in honor classes. You couldn't help but notice this. I have spent many years almost ashamed of being Mexican. It's almost as if I believed that being Latina meant being stupid and lazy. Now that I know better it upsets me to have been ashamed for so many years. I'm angry that I had to hide who I was to fit in.

3. I always thought that school would be a place to get an education and a better understanding of the world. Yet, one understanding I got was that Mexicans were a burden to society. I don't know how I got the idea, but maybe it started when my kindergarten teacher had a language barrier with my mom that frustrated her or maybe it was my sixth grade sub who laughed at my name and paid no attention to me, when I tried to correct her. Or maybe it was the other children's look of disappointment when I told them that my mom was born in Mexico. I do not know where it all started, but I do know that my hate for my own Hispanic identity grew as my years passed in school.

Newly arrived immigrants and children who are struggling with English are particularly susceptible to ridicule and marginalization at the hands of their peers. Experiences of this nature aren't just emotionally searing. They also undermine the social and academic development of this most vulnerable population of students.

1. My middle school had very few Latinos. I felt lonely, unaccepted and misunderstood because of the huge language barrier. I rarely participated in class because my classmates called me names and excluded me from group activities. They immediately assumed I was not capable

of doing the work and rejected me. I was known as the "dumb" Mexican girl. For my experiences during class, I didn't want to go to school. I developed a low self-esteem. As I got older, I realized that I was not alone; there were others like me who didn't know English and also felt discriminated.

2. The big problem is not the school, but the kids themselves that can be very cruel at times and make you feel small because you might speak a different language or because your English is not perfect.

3. I started school in this country knowing very little English. My older sister spoke English but my parents only allowed us to speak Spanish at home. When the time came for me to start school, I only knew a few words in English that I had learned watching Sesame Street. My first days were very difficult. I didn't know anybody and, what's worse, my teacher didn't know any Spanish. I was very shy and I was afraid of being alone in school. I remember that some girls in the class didn't like me. I remember one in particular who had the same name as me, Susana. That first week of class Susana made life unpleasant for me. She pinched me. She laughed at me when I didn't understand the teacher. She took my lunch. But since I didn't speak English, I couldn't even tell the teacher what was happening to me.

How do schools deal with these kinds of situations? The following narrative describes a common scenario whereby help-seeking signals by Latino children are dismissed or minimized. Thus, children who seek help end up being doubly victimized, first by the original act of aggression and then by the indifference of the adults who are supposed to put a stop to such aggression. Left to fend for themselves under difficult circumstances, these students are particularly at risk of failure.

I was not brought up to see that there was a difference between the races and I was very naive to the fact that my classmates were upper middle class and I was not. In school, I was categorized as an ESL student at a very young age for the mere fact I was Latina. There was a definite culture barrier and trying to explain to my father that all my friends' parents went to PTA meetings was difficult. I think I experienced prejudice and racial slurs but never really understood these problems until 5th grade. That's when I decided to run for student body president. Little did I know that this decision would forever alter my perception of the world and myself. Jessica, the girl that ran against me, came from what seemed to be the perfect family. Her father was a well-known doctor and the mother was the head of the PTA. I had no fear of the elections because I truly believed in myself and knew that I could lead the student body. I had passion and drive; I was unstoppable. . . . When I learned that I had not won. I started to sob uncontrollably and I wanted to run away. Not because I had lost, but because of what I heard a kid behind me say. The words are forever engraved in my memory: "It's great Jessica won. I didn't want a Mexican girl to be our president." How could someone be so cruel? My mother tried to console me, but I never told her the real reason why I couldn't stop crying. The sad thing is that I told a teacher about the situation and she just told me that they didn't mean it and walked away. The hurt has never gone away completely but I will never again allow myself to feel inferior as I did that one day in 5th grade. I will only look to the future. I will succeed and prove them all wrong.

The following comments connect the dots between a negative school climate and the rejection of school by Latino children. The experiences recounted bring to mind those of Ana and Isbelda, in particular, the pain and humiliation of receiving a bad grade from an insensitive teacher and the sense of desperation that leads to feigning illness and other tactics to avoid school.

1. The first two weeks of school were hell. I felt so out of place because I didn't understand anything anyone told me. When they'd talk they'd get real close to my face and speak slower as if I would understand them better. But that didn't help. Every day for the next month I cried all the way home and tried everything not to go to school. I lied to my parents telling them I was sick. I would stick my finger down my throat. I would hide the car keys so we would be late. I tried many things. I began learning English but then we had our first test. I remember seeing that test with a big red F. The teacher told us to read our grade out loud in alphabetical order. I felt my heart drop. I wanted to cry then and there. But I didn't.

2. When I arrived in this country, English seemed impossible to master. I had to learn so many words and the letters stood for so many different sounds. At some point, I started pretending that my stomach hurt, or my head, or other parts of my body. I didn't see the point of going to school, if I couldn't follow what was going on.

THE TREATMENT OF SPANISH

The situation surrounding Spanish in schools ranges from incomprehension and neglect to outright hostility. Fueling much of the hostility is the belief that Spanish and Latino culture get in the way of learning English and being a "real American". Ironically, as the first student points out, it is this hostility—and not Spanish and Latino culture per se—that undercuts learning and leads to subtractive schooling.

1. I had one professor that always gave me awful looks when we would have group discussions and I would discuss in Spanish with those in my group who spoke Spanish like me. I had to change that class because I couldn't learn under those conditions.

2. When I was in the third grade I had a teacher who didn't like her students speaking Spanish in class. She would punish them in front of the class when they would speak Spanish. She had the notion that in this country a person shouldn't speak anything but English. At that age I didn't know she was wrong.

Incomprehension, neglect, and hostility are particularly objectionable in Spanish classes, the area of the curriculum where Latinos' bilingual skills should be validated and their potential to enrich the labor force be nurtured. Unfortunately, this potential is undercut by a now familiar problem: instructors and counselors who lack the training to properly assess Latino students and follow up with the proper educational plan.

Mirroring what happens in the ELL track, Latino children are assumed to speak Spanish fluently solely on the basis of their looks or last name and told to enroll in advanced Spanish classes, without regard to their wishes and/or skill level. Once in these classes, however, they are criticized by their teachers and peers if their language skills are not up to the task. On the other hand, if their language skills are better than average, they risk being seen as lazy and out to get an easy A.

1. When I was in Kindergarten, my school judged me by my last name and wanted to put me in a Spanish-speaking only class. They (the school) sent a letter home to my mom telling her about the experience I would get if she signed me up for that class. My mom went to talk to the school to see why I had received that letter and the school told her that my last name was a Hispanic last name so I would have to join that class. Later in high school I had a very similar experience when I signed up

for a Spanish class. My counselor said that I would have to take Spanish for native speakers. I could not take a native-speakers class because I did not know Spanish well. I barely knew what the basics were and so I decided to take Spanish for beginners for I still had a lot to learn.

2. I am not in control of my own identity. Other people are making decisions based upon the way I speak or maybe even my appearance, and those decisions stand firm. I am not a native-speaker by any definition. My only experiences with Spanish were two and a half years of high school Spanish, a week in Mexico visiting family, and occasionally speaking Spanish with my Latino peers. I enrolled in [Intermediate Spanish] to fulfill the requirements of my Chicano Studies Degree. When I arrived to try and add the course, the teacher did some exercises in Spanish and then later told me I had to take [Spanish for Bilinguals]. I tried to explain my situation but the teacher said she had enough experience with native-speakers looking for easy "A"s to know. I am now in a situation where my academic career hangs in the balance of a class (Spanish for Bilinguals) I am very certain it's too advanced for me. This is very intimidating, but mostly it's disturbing that knowing a few words of Spanish and having a Spanish last name has sealed my fate in school.

Ironically, Latinos who actually speak Spanish are sometimes steered away from AP or honors classes in Spanish on the premise that they do not need further instruction. This is akin to saying that native English speakers do not benefit from taking AP or honors English classes. Latinos are also steered away from such classes on the premise that they will have an unfair advantage over non-Latinos. This is akin to keeping students with musical training from joining their school band because they will know more than their nontrained peers. To further the irony, in the following comment, it is a Latina counselor who gives this misguided advice.

I did not have the opportunity to take Spanish in high school because my counselor, who was a Latina, would only allow non-Latinos to take AP Spanish.

In fact, AP and honors Spanish classes can give Latino students the type of rigorous academic training and confidence-building experiences that they frequently miss out on as a result of academic profiling, not to mention help them develop skills that can translate into social and professional opportunities down the line. In addition, as explained in the following text, these classes can help boost students' academic record.

The thought of learning French was something that had crossed my mind. But the thought of an A+ on my report card next to "AP Spanish" was a better vision. Having the ability of knowing this language and the advantage of having Spanish-speaking parents did help me get a good grade in the class, a B. It sure wasn't an A+, but I was still happy with this grade.

Completing the picture of the no-win situation that many Latinos are up against with regard to Spanish, the following student is ridiculed for not speaking proper Spanish and criticized for choosing to study French. It's easy to imagine that the opposite choice—that is, choosing Spanish over French instead—would have also met with criticism and ridicule.

I visited my friend's Spanish class and although the teacher was nice, he assumed I knew proper Spanish and when I spoke improperly, he laughed at me and made me feel bad for not choosing to improve my Spanish by taking French in high school.

The contradictions surrounding Spanish in the school context have correlates outside of school. We examine these in detail in Chapters 2 and 3, which focus on language and culture, respectively.

POVERTY, SEGREGATION, AND LINGUISTIC ISOLATION

Many Latinos attend schools in impoverished urban areas where they have to contend with a daunting number of challenges that undermine their ability to get ahead in school. Calling attention to one particularly serious challenge, the chilling comment by a student from an impoverished neighborhood that he used to receive more gang invites than college fliers reminds us that gang violence does not just represent a physical threat to youth but also represents a formidable threat to their academic development.

In elementary school I was in bilingual education until California Proposition 227 banned it. I used to be teased as a kid for my thick accent until sixth grade when I became one of the tallest kids in the school. In middle school I used to look up to my cousin who was older by two years. He was a cool guy and would let me know what to prepare for. All that changed when he joined a local gang following the footsteps of an older uncle. As soon as he began his criminal activity I no longer tagged along with him as I knew I might be pressured to do the same and my father would not have it. Instead, I joined a college prep program. When it came time to apply to high school, it came down to two schools. Being more concerned with distance than the reputation of the schools, I decided to go to [the second school]; an overcrowded high school with a diverse student body consisting of 60% Latinos, 30% Black and 10% Asian and Pacific Islanders. This school had a serious gang problem. I tried to stay away from them, but that changed midway through my first semester there. The sudden change came one day after school when I was walking home and a gang jumped me two blocks from my home. They kept hitting me until finally one of them took my wallet and my money. From there, I started to associate with a few acquaintances that were in gangs out of fear of being beaten up again. I heard of various similar incidents of Black gangs preying on Latino students and Latino gangs preying on Blacks, regardless of whether they were in gangs or not. Tensions escalated so much that during that year two full-blown race riots broke out, which forced the local police to intervene. I knew right from wrong and a teacher followed me closely during that year to make sure that I didn't go off track. My parents did the same at home. Weekly I would receive more gang invites than college fliers, but I stayed on task even when it was very tempting to go off track. By my senior year most gang problems had ceased and life was far more mellow. But then I caught a bad case of senioritis. I became so comfortable that school work was not on my agenda and I was failing half of my classes. I knew that if I kept going that way I would not graduate and colleges would reject my admission. The same teacher that helped me during my gang days reminded me how much I had gone through and followed me closely again so that I would concentrate on my studies. That last semester of high school I worked so hard that I passed every class and graduated on time. Out of a senior class of almost 900 students, only 225 graduated.

While this student managed to beat the odds, it is striking that the large majority of his schoolmates did not. According to a recent study, children from disadvantaged neighborhoods are substantially less likely to graduate from high school.[38] Quantifying the effects of poverty on academic outcomes, education experts Michael Rebell and Jessica Wolff note:

America does not have a general education crisis; we have a poverty crisis. Results of an international student assessment indicate that U.S. schools with fewer than 25 percent of their students living in poverty rank first in the world among advanced industrial countries. But when you add in the scores of students from schools with high poverty rates, the United States sinks to the middle of the pack.[39]

Students who do manage to graduate and go on to college frequently struggle with academic deficiencies resulting from any number of conditions associated with schools in impoverished neighborhoods, including larger class sizes, poor facilities, and reduced access to qualified teachers, high-quality materials, and academically accelerated programs.[40] The following student's experience serves as a reminder that the seeds of poverty, planted early in life, continue to bear bitter fruit for Latino students throughout their academic careers, including college:

> Upon entry to the university, I was placed into remedial classes for English and mathematics, even though I did well in all my English and math classes in high school. But historically, I, along with many of my high school companions, performed below our true potential on standardized tests. I guess in a way, being a Chicano or Latino in a low-income minority community caused me to attend a less-than-great high school, which, in a way, may have handicapped me due to the lack of resources in our school.

Many schools in high-poverty areas are also highly segregated, in the sense that they enroll a disproportionately large number of language minority students for whom English is a second language. As a result, language minority students find themselves in a state of linguistic isolation, which affords them few opportunities to hone their English skills through interactions with native English-speaking children.[41]

The following students address another downside of segregation: the cultural shock experienced by youth upon first coming into contact with the mainstream English-speaking world. For some, this contact comes relatively early in life while for others, including the following students, as late as college. In all cases, this contact is fraught with personal quandaries about identity, language competence, and their ability to fit in. These comments, along with others in this chapter, also serve as a reminder that the climate of neglect, insensitivity, and hostility persists through higher education.

1. Having been raised in a city where Mexicans or Hispanics are the majority, I have never once felt that I was a minority. It is only when I step into places like [the university] that I feel like a minority. In the

year 2006 when our two governments (American and Mexican) argue about expanding border controls to keep all the "aliens" away, it makes me feel like an alien even though my parents legally crossed the border back in the 1970s. Being born in Los Angeles makes me as much an American as any other person in America. It is only when I am back in my community, Mi Patria, that I feel I'm in the land of the free.

2. Coming from a 99% Latino high school and community, I never felt less of a person from speaking Spanish. All that changed in college, where it's really hard to communicate deeply with anyone because people either don't understand Spanish or just care less about Spanish speakers. I had one professor that always gave me awful looks when I would speak Spanish to my classmates who were also Hispanic. I had to drop that class because I couldn't learn under those conditions.

3. I felt extremely unwelcome and not at home initially when I arrived at college. All I saw was Caucasian students (there were only two students of Caucasian descent in my high school).

TAPPING RESOURCES AND CREATING OPPORTUNITIES

If the student comments in the previous sections speak to the half of the glass that is empty, those featured in the remaining sections of this chapter direct our attention to the half that is full. Near the beginning of this chapter, in the context of discussing Patricia Gándara's statement that "the most urgent problem for the American Education system has a Latino face,"[42] we made the claim that the greatest potential for the American education system also has a Latino face. In the final sections of this chapter, we examine this assertion more closely.

Latino youth's appraisal of their schooling experience is not limited to a list of grievances: it also includes important insights on the ingredients of additive schooling. Many of the insights and suggestions featured in this section are well known in the research literature. What makes them valuable in this context is that they speak to the wisdom and perceptiveness of Latino youth regarding their situation, and, more broadly, regarding what it takes to become an educated person. In so doing, these comments are a testament to the potential of Latino youth and a reminder to teachers and other adults that these youths as more than just a problem—they are also go-to experts on issues of schooling.

Our students identify two particularly important elements of additive schooling: caring teachers and a supportive school environment.

Quantifying the importance of these conditions, one recent study found that youth who strongly agreed with the statements (1) "I have at least one teacher who makes me feel excited about the future" and (2) "My school is committed to building the strengths of each student" are 30 times more likely to be academically engaged than students who strongly disagree with those statements.[43] Like many of the narratives in this section, the study speaks to the importance of building hope.

In his memoir *Burro Genius,* best-selling novelist Victor Villaseñor describes the crushing effects of being mistreated and underestimated by his English teacher. Many years later, those experiences continue to gnaw at him, eroding his self-esteem and provoking pain. Powerful as they are, however, these experiences are no match for the impact of one caring adult—a substitute teacher—who briefly comes into his life and, recognizing his talent, unleashes the writer in him, with life-altering consequences. Describing this impact, Villaseñor notes:

> I was double, triple, quadruple SHOCKED! I'd never had an A in all my life! My heart was beat, beat, beating a million miles an hour! . . . I remembered all this like it had happened in a far away, foggy dream. My God, I really hadn't realized it, but I owed so much of my joy of reading and writing to that substitute teacher in the seventh grade who, in three tiny days, had touched my heart and soul. . . . He'd cut across the valleys of my deepest doubts, giving light to the darkest crevices of my beaten-down, inhibited mind, accessing a natural storytelling ability within me that was utterly profound![44]

Our students describe equally transformative experiences made possible by caring and talented teachers.

1. When I entered first grade, my teacher was an angel. I still remember her until this day. She would stay with me during recess, lunch and sometimes after school in order for me to better my understanding of English. By third grade, I was at the top of the class. I made a complete 180-degree turn. I learned the language very quickly and became a lover of reading. I read all day if I could. My fifth grade teacher gave me the novel *The Great Gatsby* as my graduation present and to this day it is my favorite novel of all time. I have had great relationships with most of my teachers especially those who impacted my life as heavily as the ones in elementary and middle school. I went back to tutor a class of third graders one summer, I think it was 5 or 6 years after I had left the school and

some of the teachers still recognized me. I wanted to help those kids who were just like me, who had the desire to learn, but needed that extra push by someone who understood where they were coming from. I loved to teach the kids lessons and I thought one day I would become a teacher.

2. Coming from an Hispanic middle school, college was something many of us didn't really think about. When I first entered high school, my goal was to graduate and become one of very few members of my family to receive a high school diploma. So there I was, going from class to class not knowing what was to become of me. All I had to do was get decent grades to make my father proud. It was in my sophomore year when I realized that I actually needed college to better myself, my family, and my community. A special teacher provided me with the tools to succeed in college. He pushed me to do my best in school. Of course, I had the support of my parents. However, it was hard for them to understand because they didn't have the same experiences as me. Throughout high school, this teacher helped me with everything, from providing me with math tutoring, to filling out applications for college and support. He also told me about the Summer Bridge Program, an intense six-week program that helps incoming freshmen succeed in college. This program taught me good study habits, time management, and other things I needed to survive in college. But for this teacher, I probably wouldn't have made it to college. As of today, I keep in touch with him and he continues to mentor students such as myself.

3. In fifth grade my school's bilingual program was eliminated. Thankfully, my teacher was a Cuban and partnered with another Latina teacher to help improve everyone's language skills through an after school program. She divided the students into three groups, bilinguals, Spanish speakers who needed to improve their English, and English speakers who needed to improve their Spanish. I was put in the bilinguals group and my teacher helped me focus on improving my Spanish by writing essays and reading Spanish-language novels and discussing them in English. By the end of elementary school I had become the school's representative for Spanish-speakers in student council.

Special school programs and learning experiences can also prove transformational. Grounded in a keen understanding of where students are coming from and driven by a soaring vision of where they can go, these programs, along with caring teachers, are key to improving Latinos' educational attainment.

The first of the following comments describes an *additive* schooling experience in an ESL class, the elements of which include a knowledge-able teacher and respectful and caring classmates. The second comment references the same program that helped Isbelda succeed in school, namely, the AVID program. This and the other programs mentioned here are briefly described in the Resources section at the end of this chapter.

1. In elementary school, my teachers often commented on how bad my English was and students made fun of the way I spoke. In junior high, I was placed in an ESL class. At first I was embarrassed because I could not be in the same English class with my friends. Some students would tell me I was retarded. I came to believe that there was something wrong with me. But, as it turned out, those classes were very helpful. The teacher and the other students really understood my needs. I really connected with these students and became so excited about the material that I became my mom and dad's English teacher, teaching them to read and write. After that course, I went back to "regular" courses, with my so-called "friends."

2. As I recall back in high school, my freshman year, I enrolled myself in a program called AVID which focused on first generation children working hard to help them receive a college education. Mr. Smith, a humble, kind man, was my angel from above pushing me and never letting me fall. In other words, he was the person that always believed I was capable of doing whatever I desired.

3. An event that was very meaningful to me was the Summer Bridge Program. This was a six-week program over the summer which helped minority students become more successful in college. This program helped me make the transition from high school to college by giving me skills to become more responsible, outgoing, cooperative, and independent. It informed of the many organizations and clubs that were available for Latinos in college. Knowing that there were many places for me to go to if I ever needed academic advising or counseling made me feel much more comfortable and less apprehensive about attending a new school.

4. Many of my friends didn't go to college because they didn't know what it was like transitioning from high school to college. The Summer Bridge helped me gain confidence and also gave me the opportunity to meet to new people. Last Winter Break, I took the opportunity to inform seniors in my high school about this program. I talked to them about my experiences in college and how this program helped me.

5. At the beginning of my sophomore year in college I started working with the California Mini Corps program. This program provides services such as tutoring and mentoring to Migrant Education students from all grade levels (K-12) in California. The majority of these students speak Spanish only or a minimal amount of English. Now that I have been working with the program for nearly three years, I can honestly say that my Spanish skills have improved dramatically. The reason why I enjoy working with the California Mini Corps is because it has made me feel comfortable in a classroom setting and has given me valuable skills such as how to create and present lesson plans to a classroom of students and how to communicate with them and enforce discipline.

Completing the recipe for additive schooling are the following suggestions and insights offered by our students. These same ideas reappear throughout this book, underscoring their importance to the success of Latino youth.

1. The best way to give Latino students a future is to make sure that they speak both of their languages well. The classification of ESL should be eliminated and Latinos should be given the same opportunities as everyone else.
2. Schools should have special programs for bilingual students that need help doing their homework. I think it's important for teachers to be bilingual or at least know a little bit to communicate with the parents. Notes that go out to parents should also be translated in Spanish so that parents know exactly what is going on with their children. Bilingual programs should be aiming for making the student fully competent in both Spanish and English.
3. I have worked with Hispanic students in a tutoring program. A lot of the material we had to work with was pretty complex, some of which I couldn't understand myself. I could not see how they expected a student who was still becoming comfortable with the language to understand it.
4. Teachers need to be taught to be culturally sensitive with Latino students. Many Latinos feel that school is not the place for them. When teachers say insensitive things or imply that they are not good enough, this only serves to further alienate Latinos.
5. In my schooling experience I only remember having two Latino teachers. Latino students should be encouraged to become teachers.

Students feel more comfortable approaching teachers they can relate to and who won't ridicule or embarrass them.

6. I don't believe it is fair to expect the same or equal level of writing capabilities for students who only speak English versus students in which English is spoken as their second language. Although standardized writing proficiency exams measure the skills to be fully certified proficient in written English, there should be a way to assess similar abilities for students who did not grow up speaking English in their homes.

7. Teaching for success can make a huge difference in a child's life. Any rude comment can scar a child and a lot of support can help a child overcome the negative.

THE PAYOFF: AN OPPORTUNITY FROM WHICH WE CAN BENEFIT

The closing narratives of this chapter highlight the payoffs for society of investing in Latinos' educational attainment and additive schooling: Latino youth who overcome obstacles and succeed in school are committed to helping others do the same. Well educated, with strong bicultural and bilingual skills, these individuals are also key to this nation's economic future, which is increasingly linked with having a multilingual workforce.[45] They are, in Eugene García's words, "an opportunity from which we can benefit."

1. As I got older, I realized that my mom was not the only parent who was in need of a translator during parent-teacher conferences. By the time I was in the 7th grade, I began volunteering for teachers to translate during parent-teacher conferences. I did this during 8th grade and throughout high school as well. This inspired other students at my high school to do the same. It felt great to be able to help so many parents get involved in their child's education and also to motivate other students to help out. I was recognized for my work during my high school senior award ceremony. I felt really honored.

2. During high school, I was a translator for my history class. I loved helping my fellow classmates. I was seen as a helpful and smart person. My instructor praised me and said that I was a valuable asset to the class and the school. That made me feel proud to speak Spanish.

3. Most of the regular curriculum is Anglo-centered. In my ethnic studies class you get the other perspective. Through many such classes I learned not only about Latino marginalization but the marginalization of other groups. Through these classes I decided that my education was more than just a mere instrument to my own personal wealth. I had always thought that I wanted to go into corporate law, but knowing what I know now, I couldn't possibly live with myself if I did that. I want to use the law to help under-represented minorities fight for their rights. So while I no longer stand to make a lot of money, I will be wealthy because I will use my education to benefit many others. I plan on studying immigration law and form my own non-profit in the future.

4. Being a Mexican American, I can help those who are not as fortunate. I can help by sharing my knowledge about the law and societal resources. This is why I chose to major in Chicano/Latino Studies. I felt that in order to help, I needed to understand the history, politics, health and education of Latinos in the US.

5. Growing up, I had to overcome numerous obstacles. Students laughed at me for not knowing proper English. My parents were not able to help me with my school work because they did not speak English. Recently, I realized that I want to teach children who face a similar experience. This is why I have joined the Teaching Credential Program at my university.

6. Eventually I want to hold an administrative position in school as I think I would want to go back and help my Latino community. Education is the greatest investment one can make, that is why I would want to be involved in the education process at an elementary school or high school.

DISCUSSION QUESTIONS

1. As explained in this chapter, to develop grade-appropriate reading and writing skills, students need to interact with texts that are conceptually and linguistically challenging and that expose them to academic English. Compare the language and coverage of the Boston Tea Party in the following LEP and mainstream texts. Consider factors such as vocabulary difficulty, average length of sentences, and the use of rhetorical and grammatical devices to connect ideas. In light of your findings, which text is better suited for students who have a grasp of conversational English but are in need of developing grade-appropriate literacy skills? Why?

LEP reading

The Tea Act of 1773

In May 1773 Parliament passed a law. It was called the Tea Act. King George wanted to help the British East India Company. The East India Company had 17 million pounds (7.65 million kilograms) of unsold tea. It was stored in English warehouses. The Tea Act said the East India Company could sell the tea to American colonists. The tea was taxed two times. It was taxed in England. Then it was taxed again in the colonies. The East India Company sent 1,700 chests of tea to the colonies. The colonists were not pleased. They did not like the tax. They did not want to buy the tea. Many people thought the king wanted to crush the colonists.

The Boston Tea Party

The ships filled with tea sailed into Boston Harbor on November 27. The colonists were angry. They would not let the tea be brought ashore. It had to stay on the ships. On December 16, some townspeople disguised themselves as Mohawks. At night, they boarded three ships. They dumped the tea chests into the harbor. The tea was worth £15,000. The people called this the Boston Tea Party.[46]

Non-LEP reading

Crisis Over Tea

By the early 1770s, some Americans considered British colonial policy a "conspiracy against liberty." The British government's actions seemed to confirm that view. In 1773 Parliament passed the Tea Act. It allowed the British East India Company to ship tea to the colonies without paying the taxes colonial tea merchants had to pay. This allowed the company to sell its tea very cheaply and threatened to drive the colonial tea merchants out of business.

In Massachusetts, angry colonists decided to take action. A group of protestors dressed as Native Americans boarded several British ships in Boston Harbor and dumped their cargoes of tea overboard, an event that became known as the Boston Tea Party. Word of this act of defiance spread throughout the colonies. Men and women gathered in the streets to celebrate.[47]

2. Page [12–13] has the schedule of three LEP students in California. Compare their course regimen to the recommendations of the California State University system for college-bound students (later). What specific gaps do you notice in the LEP schedules? If you were their guidance counselor or teacher, what would you do to ensure that these students are prepared for college?

California State University–recommended courses for high school students:[48]

English: Four years of college preparatory English composition and literature (take one each year)

Math: Three years (four years are recommended), including Algebra I, Geometry, Algebra II, or higher mathematics (take one each year)

History and Social Science: Two years, including one year of U.S. History (or one semester of U.S. History and one semester of Civics or American Government) and one year of Social Science

Laboratory Science: Two years with a lab class

Language (other than English): Two years of the same language (American Sign Language is applicable) (three years recommended)

Visual and Performing Arts: One year of dance, drama or theater, music, or visual arts

College Preparatory Elective: One year of any college preparatory subject

3. Previewing a key concept developed in Chapters 3 and 4, some students in this chapter manifest *resilience*—the capacity to tap into personal, cultural, and social resources for maintaining well-being and finding meaning under difficult situations. Choose one or two narratives and analyze how resilience is manifested. Consider the following personal strengths that are associated with resilience: (1) social competence, which includes responsiveness, cross-cultural communication skills, empathy and caring, forgiveness, altruism; (2) problem solving, which includes planning, flexibility, resourcefulness, critical consciousness, and insights; (3) autonomy, which includes positive identity, self-efficacy and mastery, adaptive distancing and resistance, self-awareness and mindfulness, humor; and (4) sense of purpose, which includes goal direction, special interest, optimism, hope, sense of meaning.[49]

ONLINE RESOURCES ON LATINOS IN AMERICAN SCHOOLS

Alliance for Excellent Education (http://www.all4ed.org)
A national advocacy group that focuses on policies that will lead to higher secondary graduation rates and students who are better prepared for college.

The California Dropout Research Project (http://cdrp.ucsb.edu)
A project of the University of California, Santa Barbara, designed to provide information on the problems associated with the dropout rate in California.

ERIC (http://www.eric.ed.gov/)

An online digital library sponsored by the U.S. Department of Education providing unlimited access to over a million journal articles on education.

National Center for Education Statistics (http://nces.ed.gov)

The primary organization within the U.S. Department of Education and Institute of Education Sciences that collects and analyzes data relating to education.

The Pew Hispanic Center (http://pewhispanic.org)

A project of the Pew Research Center that publishes studies and surveys on a range of issues pertaining to U.S. Latinos, including education.

Spotlight on Educational Excellence (http://www.nclr.org)

An initiative of the National Council of La Raza focusing on issues, policy, and practices of relevance to the education of Latino children.

U.S. Department of Education (http://www.ed.gov)

A federal website that publishes a wide variety of education-related information, including educational statistics, grants, and teacher resources.

The White House Initiative on Educational Excellence for Hispanic Americans (http://www.ed.gov/edblogs/hispanic-initiative/)

An initiative to give "advice to the Secretary of Education on the progress of Hispanic Americans toward achievement of national education goals and on such other aspects of the educational status of Hispanic Americans as it consider[ed] appropriate."

Programs That Work

AVID (Advancement Via Individual Determination) (http:// avid.org)

A nationwide program that focuses on helping traditionally underrepresented students attend a four-year university directly after high school graduation.

The Puente Project (http://www.Puente.net)

An interdisciplinary California project designed to increase college attendance among educationally disadvantaged students.

Summer Bridge Program (contact individual universities for details)

A nationwide program that provides academic services and an introduction to university life to incoming first-year students the summer prior to enrollment.

The Gates Millennium Scholars (https://www.gmsp.org)

One thousand good-through-graduation scholarships available for African American, American Indian/Alaska Native, Asian Pacific Islander American, or Hispanic American students with personal and professional development through along with academic support throughout their college career.

Excelencia in Education (http://edexcelencia.org/)

A website that uses data and analysis as a means of applying knowledge to public policy and institutional practice.

NOTES

1. Richard Fry, "Latinos in Higher Education: Many Enroll, Too Few Gradu-ate." *Pew Hispanic Center,* 2002. September 5, 2002. http://www.pewhispanic .org/2002/09/05/latinos-in-higher-education

2. "Indicators of School Crime and Safety: 2007: Indicator 17." *National Center for Education Statistics, U.S. Department of Education,* n.d. http://nces .ed.gov/programs/crimeindicators/crimeindicators2007/ind_17.asp.

3. "Status Dropout Rates." National Center for Education Statistics, U.S. Department of Education, January 2014. http://nces.ed.gov/programs/coe/indica tor_coj.asp.

4. Richard Fry and Mark Hugo Lopez, "Hispanic Student Enrollments Reach New Highs in 2011: Now Largest Minority Group on Four-Year College Campuses." *Pew Hispanic Center,* August 20, 2012. http://www.pewhispanic .org/2012/08/20/hispanic-student-enrollments-reach-new-highs-in-2011/.

5. Ibid.

6. Ibid.

7. Richard Fry and Felisa Gonzales, "One in Five and Growing Fast: A Profile of Hispanic Public School Students." *Pew Hispanic Center,* August 26, 2008. http:// www.pewhispanic.org/2008/08/26/one-in-five-and-growing-fast-a-profile-of-hispanic-public-school-students/.

8. Fry and Lopez, "Hispanic Student Enrollments Reach New Highs in 2011: Now Largest Minority Group on Four-Year College Campuses."

9. Robert Samuels, "With Hispanic Students on the Rise, Hispanic Teach-ers in Short Supply." *The Washington Post,* November 15, 2011, sec. Education. http://www.washingtonpost.com/local/education/with-hispanic-students-on-the-rise-hispanic-teachers-in-short-supply/2011/11/01/gIQASFkbPN_story .html.

10. Fry and Gonzales, "One in Five and Growing Fast: A Profile of Hispanic Public School Students."

11. Ibid.

12. Mark Hugo Lopez, "Latinos and Education: Explaining the Attain-ment Gap." *Pew Hispanic Center,* October 7, 2009. http://www.pewhispanic .org/2009/10/07/latinos-and-education-explaining-the-attainment-gap/.

13. Fry and Gonzales, "One in Five and Growing Fast: A Profile of Hispanic Public School Students."

14. Ibid.

15. Ibid.

16. Lopez, "Latinos and Education: Explaining the Attainment Gap."

17. Ibid.

18. Ibid.

19. Fry and Lopez, "Hispanic Student Enrollments Reach New Highs in 2011: Now Largest Minority Group on Four-Year College Campuses."

20. Richard Fry, "Hispanic College Enrollment Spikes, Narrowing Gaps with Other Groups." *Pew Hispanic Center*, August 25, 2011. http://www.pewhispanic.org/2011/08/25/hispanic-college-enrollment-spikes-narrowing-gaps-with-other-groups/.

21. "Status Dropout Rates." *National Center for Education Statistics, U.S. Department of Education*, January 2014. http://nces.ed.gov/programs/coe/indicator_coj.asp.

22. Ibid.

23. *Listening to Latinas: Barriers to School Graduation—Executive Summary.* National Women's Law Center & Mexican American Legal Defense and Educational Fund, June 9, 2009.

24. "How California's Dropout Crisis Affects Communities." *California Dropout Research Project*, n.d. http://cdrp.ucsb.edu/dropouts/pubs_cityprofiles.htm.

25. Patricia Gándara, "The Crisis in the Education of Latino Students." *NEA Research Visiting Scholars Series* 1a, no. Spring 2008 (n.d.). http://www.nea.org/home/17404.htm.

26. Eugene García, *Hispanic Education in the United States. Raíces y Alas.* Oxford: Rowman & Littlefield, 2001.

27. Fry, "Hispanic College Enrollment Spikes, Narrowing Gaps with Other Groups."

28. "How California's Dropout Crisis Affects Communities."

29. John Amos, *Dropouts, Diplomas, and Dollars U.S. High Schools and the Nation's Economy.* Alliance for Excellent Education, August 2008. http://www.doe.virginia.gov/support/prevention/dropout_truancy/resources/dropouts_diplomas_dollars.pdf.

30. Angela Valenzuela, *Subtractive Schooling: U.S.-Mexican Youth and the Politics of Caring.* October 2, 1999. Albany: State University of New York Press, 1999.

31. Fry and Gonzales, "One in Five and Growing Fast: A Profile of Hispanic Public School Students."

32. Howard L. Fleischman, Paul J. Hopstock, Todd G. Stephenson, Michelle L. Pendzick, and Saloni Sapru. *Descriptive Study of Services to LEP Students and LEP Students with Disabilities.* Vol. 4. U.S. Department of Education, Office of English Language Acquisition, Language Enhancement, and Academic Achievement for Limited English Proficient Students, 2003.

33. Lily Wong Fillmore and Catherine Snow, *What Teachers Need to Know about Language.* ERIC Clearinghouse on Languages and Linguistics, n.d. http://files.eric.ed.gov/fulltext/ED447721.pdf.

34. Patricia Gándara, R. Rumberger, J. Maxwell-Jolly, and R. Callahan, "English Learners in California Schools: Unequal Resources, Unequal Outcomes." Edited by Gene V. Glass. *Education Policy Analysis Archives* 11, no. 36 (October 7, 2003).

35. Gilda Ochoa, *Academic Profiling. Latinos, Asian Americans and the Achievement Gap.* Minneapolis: University of Minnesota Press, 2013.

36. Ofelia García and Jo Anne Kleifgen, *Educating Emergent Bilinguals. Policies, Programs, and Practices for English Language Learners.* New York: Language and Literacy Series. Teachers College Press, 2010.

37. Frederick Williams, "Some Research Notes on Dialect Attitudes and Stereotypes." In *Variation in the Form and Use of Language: A Sociolinguistics Reader,* edited by Ralph Fasold, 354–69. Washington, DC: Georgetown University Press, 1984.

38. Geffrey T. Wodtke, David J. Harding, and Felix Elwert, "Neighborhood Effects in Temporal Perspective." *American Sociological Review* 76, no. 5 (October 1, 2011): 723–36. http://www.ncbi.nlm.nih.gov/pubmed/22879678?dopt= Ab stract.

39. Michael Rebell and Jessica R. Wolff, "We Can Overcome Poverty's Impact on School Success." *Education Week,* January 17, 2012, sec. Commentary. http://www.edweek.org/ew/articles/2012/01/18/17rebell.h31.html?tkn=OSMFeVuUEJ K7KsyeTYKBRMZ27cyO6y2uXVX%2B&cmp=ENL-EU-VIEWS1.

40. Patricia Gándara, Russell Rumberger, Julie Maxwell-Jolly, and Rebecca Callahan, Rebecca, "English Learners in California Schools: Unequal resources, Unequal Outcomes." *Education Policy Analysis Archives,* 11 (36) (2003). Website: http://epaa.asu.edu/epaa/v11n36/.

41. García and Kleifgen, *Educating Emergent Bilinguals. Policies, Programs, and Practices for English Language Learners.*

42. Gándara, "The Crisis in the Education of Latino Students."

43. Evie Blad, "Poll: Majority of Students 'Engaged.'" *Education Week,* April 16, 2014. http://www.edweek.org/ew/articles/2014/04/09/28gallup.h33.html.

44. Victor Villaseñor, *Burro Genius: A Memoir.* New York: Harper Perrenial, 2005.

45. "Reducing the Impact of Language Barriers." *Forbes,* September 2011. http://www.forbes.com/forbesinsights/language_study_reg/index.html; Forbes Insight & Rosetta Stone. (2011). "Reducing the impact of language barriers." *Forbes.* Retrieved from www.forbes.com/forbesinsights.

46. Lily Wong Fillmore and Catherine E. Snow, *What Teachers Need to Know about Language.* U.S. Department of Education's Office of Educational Research and Improvement. ERIC, August 23, 2000.

47. Joyce Appleby, Alan Brinkley, Albert Broussard, James McPherson, and Donald Ritchie, *The American Journey.* New York: McGraw-Hill, 2006.

48. The California State University. "How to Get to College." *California State University,* n.d. http://www.calstate.edu/college.

49. Michael Ungar, "Resilience across Cultures." *British Journal of Social Work* 38 (2008): 218–35.

TWO

Voces about Language

In Chapter 1, we examined issues of language in the context of school. In this chapter, we revisit such issues, broadening the picture to American society and the world at large. With nearly one out of every five U.S. residents speaking a language other than English at home, questions surrounding immigrant languages figure prominently in the public discourse. Among such questions are the following: Aren't immigrant children better served by leaving their home language behind? Aren't we better off as a country with English as our only language? Why are today's immigrants not learning English?

As the most spoken immigrant language in this country, Spanish often takes center place in discussions concerning these and other questions. Unfortunately, mirroring what happens in schools, misperceptions and biases sometimes confuse the issues and get in the way of a constructive discussion. This situation ultimately hurts Latino children and society at large. To understand why, it's worth considering an example of bias, taken to the extreme. The following piece, by _Vanity Fair_ columnist Dame Edna, was in response to a reader's inquiry about the value of learning Spanish: "Forget Spanish. There's nothing in that language worth reading except Don Quixote. . . . There was a poet named García Lorca, but I'd leave him on the intellectual back burner if I were you. As for everyone's speaking it, what twaddle! Who speaks it that you are really desperate to talk to? The help?"[1]

With a rich literary tradition spanning hundreds of years, Spanish has many masterpieces, well worth reading, including those of 11 Nobel Prize–winning authors whose names are listed at the end of this chapter. It is also a major world language, on par with English, Mandarin, French, and so forth. An official language in 20 countries with over 500 million speakers worldwide,[2] it is the language of many highly educated people, including doctors, lawyers, engineers, educators, and so on.

But even if we assume for the sake of discussion that Dame Edna is correct about Spanish being only for help, would this make this language not worth learning and its speakers not worth interacting with? What are the children of service employees to make of her advice, that they should be ashamed of their parents and abandon their home language? And what about the rest of society, that the language of 50 million people in this country does not merit any attention? Dame Edna's comments, and *Vanity Fair*'s willingness to publish them, speak to the serious nature of the misconceptions surrounding the Spanish language and its speakers in the United States.

To be fair, it is important to note that U.S. Latinos themselves are not above making such judgments about their own language, as illustrated by the following student comment:

To me, the Spanish language has never connoted intelligence. None of my family members and other adults who lived here and surrounded me had any more than a third grade education. The Spanish they speak, which is the one that I learned to speak, is not the most proper. I grew up not knowing or being around educated Spanish speakers. It was only when I began to read Spanish books that I realized that Spanish can be intelligent.

How can this be? Dame Edna's explicit connection between Spanish and service sector workers and the student's mention of uneducated Spanish speakers provide a clue. Linguistic research shows that value judgments about language are usually based on social evaluations of its speakers. In essence, the language of high-prestige groups is judged positively, while that of low-prestige groups is condemned.[3] With high poverty rates, low levels of education, and limited political clout, Latinos, as a group, rank low on the social scale. It follows that Spanish does too.

With this and other linguistic realities in mind, one of our primary goals for this chapter is to bring the insights of history, linguistic science, and Latino youth to bear on discussions surrounding the place of Spanish in American society and in the lives of U.S. Latinos. Another is to shed light on the strategies invoked by Latino youth for reaping the rewards of knowing two languages in a society that is not generally supportive of their bilingualism. As author Ilan Stavans observes: "Curiously in the United States, to be a member of the upper class and a polyglot is a ticket to success. But multilingualism among the poor is unacceptable and, thus, immediately condemned."[4]

The overview at the beginning of the chapter describes the status of Spanish in the world and the historical circumstances that brought this language to our shores and led up to its current situation. Against this backdrop, the voices in this chapter open a window to the complex linguistic universe inhabited by Latino youth. In this universe, Spanish is both ally and foe, a badge of honor and a stain of shame, a major player among world languages and a ghetto language. Along with these voices, we feature numerous quotes by prominent Latinos addressing different aspects of this experience.

What sets these experiences apart and occupies our attention in this chapter is that so many of them are rooted in the disapproval of others—from family members to teachers, public figures, and even strangers on the street. These experiences contrast with those of mainstream members of society, which linguist Rosina Lippi-Green describes as follows:

> As a speaker of a variety of US English which is not stigmatized, on occasion I feel inferior about my own language. . . . But because I belong to the social (and hence, to the language) mainstream which isolates me from the process of subordination, any feelings of inferiority are my own making. Other value systems are not forced on me. I am allowed the consolation of my mother tongue. *I am free of the shadow of language, and subject only to the standards that I accept for myself* (emphasis ours).[5]

To those who share Professor Lippi-Green's background, the experiences relayed in this chapter will reveal an unknown parallel universe—one where Latino children find themselves under the shadow of not one, but two languages. How they maneuver and rise above the challenges of this universe is well worth our attention.

SPANISH BY THE NUMBERS

Spanish in the World[6]

500 million:	Number of Spanish speakers in the world, including native and nonnative speakers
20:	Number of countries where Spanish is an official language
8.52:	Percentage of Internet users in the world who speak Spanish, making this the third most popular language in the Internet after English and Chinese
7.29:	Percentage of the world population that speaks Spanish, including first- and second-language speakers
6:	Number of official languages of the United Nations, one of them being Spanish

Spanish in the United States[7]

50 million: Number of Spanish speakers in the United States, including Latinos and non-Latinos

35.5 million: Number of U.S. residents over age five who use Spanish as a primary language at home

75:   Percentage of U.S. Latinos who speak Spanish at home

16:   Number of U.S. states with half a million or more Spanish speakers (Arizona, California, Colorado, Florida, Georgia, Illinois, Massachusetts, Nevada, New Jersey, New Mexico, New York, North Carolina, Pennsylvania, Texas, Virginia, and Washington)

4:   Number of states where at least one in five residents speaks Spanish at home (Arizona, California, New Mexico, and Texas)

6 million: Number of people who study Spanish in the United States every year, making this the most studied foreign language in this country[8]

1,300:   Number of Spanish-language newspapers in the United States[9]

800:   Number of Spanish-language radio stations in the United States[10]

5:   Number of Spanish-language television networks in the United States[11]

Spanish in the World

Spanish is a Romance language, which means that it evolved from Latin, the language of the Roman Empire. French, Italian, Portuguese, and Romanian are also part of the Romance family, along with lesser-known languages, such as Catalan and Galician, spoken in northern Spain, and Romansh, in Switzerland. Much like siblings, Romance languages all bear close resemblance to each other by virtue of their shared parentage.

Originally spoken in the northern part of what is modern-day Spain, Spanish first rose to prominence during the reign of Isabella of Castile and Fernando of Aragón, who declared it the official language of their kingdom in 1492. Over the next centuries, Spanish explorers and colonists transported it to the Americas and other parts of the world, giving rise to its current status as a major world language.

Today, Spanish is the second most spoken language in the world (after Mandarin), as measured by numbers of native speakers, and the fourth most spoken language in total speakers (including first- and second-language speakers), after Chinese, Hindi, and English.[12] In all, 7.29 percent of the world's population speaks Spanish, either as a first or second language. Table 2.1 lists the countries or territories where Spanish is a national language, in descending numbers of speakers.[13] Table 2.2 lists countries or territories where Spanish does not have official status but where 10 percent or more of the population speaks it. Of these, the United States has the largest population of speakers, in terms of raw numbers, though not in terms of percentage of speakers, relative to the overall population. Spanish also has official status in some of the largest and most important international organizations, including the European Union, the United Nations, the International Monetary Fund, the World Bank, Amnesty International, Interpol, Doctors without Borders, and the Red Cross.[14]

Table 2.1   Countries and territories where Spanish is a national language, listed in descending numbers of speakers

1. Mexico
2. Spain
3. Colombia
4. Argentina
5. Venezuela
6. Peru
7. Chile
8. Ecuador
9. Guatemala
10. Cuba
11. Dominican Republic
12. Bolivia
13. Honduras
14. El Salvador
15. Nicaragua
16. Costa Rica
17. Paraguay
18. Uruguay
19. Panama
20. Equatorial Guinea

Table 2.2   Spanish-speaking countries or territories where Spanish does not have official status

	Population That Speaks Spanish (%)
Aruba	75.3
Andorra	68.7
Dutch Antilles	56.1
Belize	42.7
Morocco	21.9
United States	16
U.S. Virgin Islands	15.5
Guam	12.3

It is important to keep in mind that most Spanish-speaking countries are multilingual and multicultural. Notably, several Romance languages are spoken in Spain, along with Basque, a language of unknown origin. For its part, Latin America is home to many indigenous and immigrant languages, including over 100 Amerindian languages in Peru and 68 in Mexico.[15]

Spanish is projected to dominate the linguistic landscape of the 21st century, along with English, Chinese, Hindi/Urdu (spoken in India), and Arabic.[16] In this regard, the United States occupies the enviable linguistic position of being home to two major world languages. The strategic advantages of this situation are particularly evident in Miami, Florida, a city that owes much of its commercial and financial success to its bilingual and bicultural identity. Dubbed "the Capital of Latin America" by *Time* magazine, it is home to the Latin American headquarters of companies such as AT&T, General Motors, Disney, and Iberia Airlines.[17]

Studies single out Spanish as particularly valuable for current business activities. Among these, a survey of graduates of the prestigious Thunderbird's Garvin School of International Management identified English and Spanish as the most useful languages at work.[18] Other fields where Spanish is in high demand include healthcare, law enforcement, education, and translation and interpretation.[19]

Not surprisingly, the study of Spanish in the United States is at an all-time high. At the high school level, it is the language of choice of an astounding 70 percent of learners. In higher education, it enrolls nearly four times more students than the next most commonly studied language, namely, French.[20] As a result, roughly a third of the 50+ million Spanish speakers in the United States are non-Latinos who learned the language at school.[21]

Altogether, these facts belie Dame Edna's comments about Spanish and speak to the opportunities alluded to by Professor Eugene García in Chapter 1, when he urges us to "marshal the intellectual resources in ways that will make the inevitable an opportunity from which we can benefit."

A BRIEF HISTORY OF SPANISH IN THE UNITED STATES

Apply yourself to the study of the Spanish language with all of the assiduity you can. It and the English covering nearly the whole of America, they should be well known to every inhabitant, who means to look beyond the limits of his farm (Thomas Jefferson, Letter to Peter Carr (1788).[22]

Thomas Jefferson's words speak to the long-standing prominence of Spanish in the Americas. This language has had a continuous presence in this country since 1513, when Juan Ponce de León, the first European to set foot in what is modern-day United States, christened his landing site *La Florida,* or "the flowery one." Soon thereafter, Spain established the first permanent European settlement in this country in St. Augustine, Florida (predating Jamestown and Plymouth Colony). At their peak, in the late 18th century, the Spanish Borderlands encompassed more than half of what is today the United States, extending along the southern rim of the country from Florida to California, and along the Pacific coast to Alaska.

Large numbers of Spanish speakers were assimilated into this country through the annexation of the Spanish Borderlands into the United States through war and land purchases. The largest increase came in 1848 at the end of the Mexican-American War when Arizona, California, Nevada, New Mexico, Texas, Utah, and parts of Colorado and Wyoming became part of the United States. It bears noting that when California became a state in 1850, it was decreed that official publications from the state would be in English and Spanish. However, this practice was discontinued a short time later.[23] Puerto Rico and Cuba were annexed at the end of the Spanish-American War in 1898. Cuba gained its independence four years later, but Puerto Rico, where Spanish is the first language, remains a U.S. territory.[24]

More recently, large numbers of Mexican workers arrived under the "Bracero" program, a temporary guest worker program created during World War II to address wartime labor shortages. Cubans arrived in various waves following the Cuban Revolution in 1959, Dominicans starting in the 1960s after the fall of the Trujillo dictatorship, and Central Americans fleeing civil unrest in the latter half of the 20th century.

In the last two decades of the 20th century and the first decade of the 21st century, political and economic turmoil in Latin America resulted in another large influx of immigrants, raising the number of Latinos in the United States from 11 million in 1980 to 40 million in 2011.[25]

U.S. SPANISH AND LATINOS IN THE 21ST CENTURY

Today, the United States is home to the second-largest population of Spanish speakers in the world, after Mexico.[26] Given the many countries of origin of U.S. Latinos, there is no single U.S. Spanish variety. Rather, different varieties of Spanish are spoken in different regions, depending on the dominant Latino population. In the Southwest, for example, Mexican varieties of Spanish are most common, while in the Northeast and Southeast, Caribbean varieties dominate. By and large, the many regional variants of Spanish have a high degree of mutual intelligibility, such that, for example, Mexicans can easily communicate with Spanish speakers from as far as Argentina or Spain.

For all the Spanish speakers in this country and for all the talk about the ever presence of Spanish in the public sphere, the fact is that this language is largely relegated to the shadows. Michele Serros, a former writer for the *George Lopez Show,* describes an experience that underscores this reality.

> Sometimes I catch reruns of The George Lopez Show on TV Land or Nick at Nite. Some episodes I find funny, hilarious. Other ones I find ho-hum. But for what it's worth, I can't help but recall how courageously George worked that first season, before he gained star power, to maintain an authentic voice for himself and for, what he believed, our community. I often felt badly as I witnessed him, the star of his own show, relegated to nearly begging for permission for any and all scraps Chicano. One time he was firmly reminded, in almost a condescending manner, that he was not to use Spanish slang. "Now George, we talked about this. There will be no Spanish." The exchange seemed like a flashback to a 1970s classroom in Texas.[27]

Contrasting with Thomas Jefferson's positive regard of Spanish, Michelle Serros's words attest to the low status of this language and its speakers in today's America. Further examples include a Dallas police officer issuing 39 traffic citations to Spanish-speaking drivers because they did not speak English,[28] a Texas judge ruling that a mother who spoke

Spanish to her child was engaging in child abuse and threatening to revoke her custodial rights,[29] a teacher hitting students for speaking Spanish in her class,[30] a school principal suspending a child for saying *no problema* to another student in a hallway before class,[31] and three women being fired because they spoke Spanish during their breaks.[32]

Behind this state of affairs is the perception that Spanish (and, to a lesser extent, other immigrant languages) represents a threat to English and national unity.[33]

This perception is not borne out by the facts. In fact, most Latinos speak English—88 percent of second-generation and 94 percent of third-generation immigrants report speaking it very well—and almost all are supportive of the idea that everyone in this country should speak English.[34] The *Pew Hispanic Center* writes: "The endorsement of the English language, both for immigrants and for their children, is strong among all Hispanics regardless of income, party affiliation, fluency in English or how long they have been living in the United States."[35]

Despite this, as of the writing of this book, 31 U.S. states have laws declaring English an official language, including California, home to the largest U.S. Latino population. California has also banned bilingual education, along with Arizona and Massachusetts, mainly out of the misplaced concern that immigrant children won't learn English or integrate into mainstream society if they receive instruction in their native tongue. Reflecting this view, the former speaker of the House of Representatives Newt Gingrich made the following recommendation: "We should replace bilingual education with immersion in English so people learn the common language of the country and so they learn the language of prosperity, not the language of living in a ghetto."[36]

In fact, research indicates that proper use of the home language in educational settings can expedite the learning of English and content knowledge (i.e., math, history, etc.) by immigrant children.[37] One advantage of Spanish in this regard is that it is relatively easy to read because of its regular orthography. As a result, many Latino children start school with basic reading skills in Spanish, having acquired them at home. This means that they can start reaping the benefits of reading at an early age, well before they are able to do so in English. The student speaks to this advantage as follows, even as he admits to rejecting Spanish in school:

In elementary school I did not want to speak Spanish, although it was the language that my parents and grandparents spoke. I first learned to read in Spanish. I read the Bible with my grandmother.

The mention of the Bible is significant for two reasons. First, being a linguistically rich and complex text, the Bible provides exposure to advanced stylistic and grammatical devices, which are not typically found in every day texts, let alone encountered in texts accessed by young children. The skills acquired in reading a text of this complexity are likely to transfer to English and contribute to the academic development of children. Second, the mention of the Bible foreshadows a discussion in Chapter 3 about the importance and value of religion in Latino homes.

The student's rejection of Spanish raises another important issue, namely, the loss of Spanish among U.S. Latinos. Research shows that knowledge of Spanish by U.S. Latinos declines across generations, which explains why a quarter of this population does not speak the language. The loss of Spanish follows a widely attested pattern for immigrant languages in the United States: the foreign-born generation (i.e., the first generation) makes wide use of the immigrant language, their children (the second generation) are bilingual with a strong preference for English, and their grandchildren (the third generation) are mostly English monolingual. Table 2.3 summarizes the results of a study of intergenerational loss of Spanish among Latinos. Notably, first-generation Latinos account for much of the Spanish heard in the United States.[38]

A second-generation Mexican American gives a firsthand account of this loss in her own family.

In Latin families Spanish is the main language for the older generations. In my family, my parents speak only Spanish. They spent their entire childhood in Mexico and moved to the U.S. after they

Table 2.3   Language dominance, by generation (Suro 2002: w13)

	Total Latinos (%)	First Generation (the Foreign Born, in %)	Second Generation (in %)	Third Generation (in %)
English dominant	25	4	46	78
Bilingual	28	24	47	22
Spanish dominant	47	72	7	–

married. Here they adapted too many things, but never the language. They've been living in this country more than 20 years and they still haven't mastered English. They understand it but don't like to speak it because they don't speak it well.

In the second generation, my generation, things are different. All my brothers and sisters, except for my twin sister and me, were born in Mexico. In all, there are six of us children and, with the exception of my oldest sister, we all speak Spanish and English very well.

The third generation is the one that experiences the most dramatic changes. For them, English is far more common than Spanish. In my family, all my nieces and nephews speak English as their first language. They understand Spanish, but they cannot speak it well. They're also far more at home with American culture than with Mexican culture.

In each generation, language changes a bit, particularly the meaning of words. Some families keep their Spanish, but some others don't. In my family Spanish hasn't been extinguished yet, but it is definitely on that path. I think it's important to keep one's language and culture. We should teach our children to speak Spanish so that it will be an integral part of their lives.

If Spanish is being lost, why does it appear to be thriving? This is because incoming immigrants from the Spanish-speaking world serve to replenish the loss of speakers from one generation to another. However, even they are not above losing their native language. Research shows that 70 percent of children arriving in the United States at the age of 10 or younger, and 40 percent of those arriving between the ages of 10 and 14, eventually lose much of their Spanish.[39]

Altogether, the facts belie the commonly held belief that Spanish is taking over English. To the contrary, it is Spanish that struggles to retain a place—even a reduced one—in the lives of Latino immigrants amid the unstoppable encroachment of English. Thus, the linguistic quandary faced by most U.S. Latinos is not whether to learn English—a language of many rewards—but rather, whether to exert any effort to retain Spanish, a language savaged by so many and with so few apparent rewards.

And still, as evidenced in Table 2.3, significant numbers of Latinos refuse to relinquish their linguistic heritage. How can that be?

Regardless of how long they've been in this country or how well they speak Spanish, most Latinos have deep emotional bonds to their mother language and culture. The students in the following text describe Spanish as the language of familial bonds, music, home-cooked meals, and protection from the glare of the outside world:

1. I was in 7th grade and Roseann was her name. I don't understand why this girl made me feel so uncomfortable. She would say "Why are you speaking Spanish We are in America, you need to speak English." That would make me feel ashamed of who I was. Coming home and listening to my música made me feel good. I sat at the dinner table and ate the frijoles and arroz (beans and rice) that my mom would make, and everything would feel great again. Roseann was not the only one who attacked me this way. There were many others who wanted to strip me of my Spanish.

2. In school, speaking Spanish was almost seen as a handicap. I was never smart enough, probably because I was underestimated and never given the opportunity to try. Early on, I learned to be silent and hide in school. My only consolation was that I knew that when I got home speaking Spanish would be beautiful. This is when I began to associate the language with love. If I were to lose my Spanish I would lose my identity and my connection to my family.

Anecdotes about being criticized for using Spanish abound in this chapter and explain why so many Latino children eventually lose this language. Some avoid using it, feeling frustrated and embarrassed by their inability to express themselves with ease. Others abandon Spanish because they come to view it as inferior to English or as an obstacle to getting ahead in school. Still others outright reject it, as a result of being shamed, shunned, or called derogatory names for speaking it. Eventually, they all forget whatever Spanish they knew, becoming monolingual in English.

This process, known as *subtractive bilingualism,* whereby the second language is added at the expense of the first language and culture, carries negative social and psychological consequences that are not fully appreciated by Latino children or their parents until after it's almost too late to change course. Blogger Chantilly Patiño describes the challenges associated with recovering Spanish, once lost:

As a family, we're facing another challenge together; how to raise a confident, bilingual, Latina daughter. Sounds easy, right? But how do you teach your child Spanish when you're not fluent yourself? How do you include Mexican heritage in your daily life when you've missed out on so much of it? How do you raise your daughter to be confident and shake off criticism when you struggle with it so much in your own life?[40]

We turn our attention to these and other issues in the context of taking inventory of the linguistic challenges faced by Latino youth.

LIFE UNDER THE SHADOW OF TWO LANGUAGES

This section draws its title and inspiration from Rosina Lippi-Green's words (reproduced next, from the beginning of this chapter). Here we examine six different linguistic burdens associated with living under the shadow of English and Spanish.

> As a speaker of a variety of U.S. English which is not stigmatized, on occasion I feel inferior about my own language. . . . But because I belong to the social (and hence, to the language) mainstream which isolates me from the process of subordination, any feelings of inferiority are my own making. Other value systems are not forced on me. I am allowed the consolation of my mother tongue. *I am free of the shadow of language, and subject only to the standards that I accept for myself* (emphasis ours).[41]

THE BURDEN OF BEING UN-AMERICAN, ANTISOCIAL, OR UNINTELLIGENT FOR SPEAKING SPANISH

As discussed in Chapter 1, speaking Spanish in school can earn a child the reputation of being unintelligent. The following comments bring to light two other perils of speaking Spanish in school, namely, being perceived as un-American and antisocial:

1. Our teacher sometimes thought we were speaking behind her back but we never did. She would ask us to stop speaking Spanish. She would say, "You're in America, speak English. Go back to Mexico if you want to speak Spanish." I started to feel I was doing something wrong to the point where I felt Spanish was inferior and would be worthless to keep up with.

2. When I was in third grade I had a teacher who didn't want her students speaking Spanish in her class. She would punish us harshly and tell us that in the U.S. we should only speak English. At that tender age, I didn't realize that she didn't know what she was speaking about.

3. I was one of only 20 Hispanics in my high school. When my best friend and I would speak Spanish, the non-Spanish speakers would look at us with anger. One day, a fellow classmate interrupted a conversation and said "Will you please stop talking about us! Why don't you

speak English and leave Spanish for the other Mexicans in Mexico." I got really offended and responded: "First of all, Mexicans are not the only ones that speak Spanish. Second, I am not Mexican, I am from Honduras. And third, what makes you think I'm talking about you? Am not even looking at you. So please, turn around and mind your own business." I couldn't believe that this girl had just labeled all Spanish speakers Mexicans.

Of course, these types of experiences are not confined to the school context, but are present in society at large. They are even present among Latinos, as attested by the following comments:

1. There was this couple where the wife was Latina and spoke Spanish. They had two girls who did not speak Spanish. When I asked them why they hadn't taught their children to speak Spanish, they answered that they didn't want them to grow up to be dishwashers. What bothered me the most is that the mom was ok with not teaching her children about her culture.

2. I remember one time in 5th grade when a boy who spoke English and Spanish put a girl down for speaking Spanish. The girls also spoke both languages but because she decided to speak Spanish, he called her a "wetback." The amazing thing is that most of us were bilingual but speaking Spanish was almost seen as being un-American.

3. Many years ago, something very unpleasant happened to my mom. I was seven years old and my brothers were four and five and my dad was still in Argentina. My mom, my brothers, and I had just arrived in San Clemente from Argentina and we were staying in a hotel while we looking for an apartment. I remember that day very clearly because my mom was very tired and frustrated. She kept calling rental offices and they would hang up on her. There was one lady in particular. My mom tried talking to her, but she kept saying . . . sorry, I don't understand and I can't help you. Feeling very frustrated, my mom asked a friend for help. He called up this lady and received a very positive response from her. They set up an appointment to see the apartment that very afternoon. I remember my mom felt relieved but also sad because of the way she had been treated for not speaking English well. When we got to the apartment, the lady who had refused to help my mom was actually speaking perfect Spanish to some workers. My mom got very angry and canceled the appointment. She told the lady that she would

never live in a place with Latinos that had forgotten where they came from and their native tongue.

4. Once I was standing in line at a store and a man asked a Latina sales lady for help in Spanish. She hesitated a moment and then answered him in English. I was astonished because I expected her to speak Spanish. The man did not understand anything and looked frustrated and embarrassed and so I decided to step in and help him. As he was leaving, he thanked me profusely for my help and commented in a loud voice that some people are so ignorant they don't deserve what they have. The saleslady stared at us, as if she had understood exactly what he had said. I looked at her and laughed.

Amid these negatives, many Latino children abandon Spanish. Those who retain this language often manage to do so by leading a double life—relegating it to the home and pretending to speak only English in school. As shown in the following text, this ruse serves different strategic purposes, from helping Latino youth blend in among their peers, to sparing them from needless instruction and testing.

1. When I started middle school I didn't want anyone to know that I spoke Spanish and was Hispanic. I couldn't hide being Hispanic, but I could avoid speaking Spanish when in school. All my friends spoke English and I didn't want to be the only one who spoke Spanish. Even when I spoke to my mom on the phone, I would speak English, and she didn't even know English very well!

2. When I was nine they gave us an English exam in school. I remember thinking it was strange, because they only gave it to the Latino children. The test was so easy that it was silly and even insulting—stuff like "draw a line, a circle. . . ." Then they asked me questions about my family. Remembering that my brother had told me that in school they didn't like people who spoke anything other than English, I told them that we spoke English at home. It was a lie, but I didn't want to be in ESL any more. I wanted to be with the rest of the students. My friend Susana's parents got angry at her because she said that her first language was Spanish and that she spoke Spanish at home. They put her in ESL because she "needed help." Ever since then, I never admitted that I spoke Spanish first. I felt bad, but that's what I had to do. And that's how I spent my years in school, pretending not to speak Spanish and watching those who spoke it being taken out of class to take stupid exams.

THE BURDEN OF NOT KNOWING SPANISH

With so many negatives associated with using Spanish, many children abandon this language, eventually losing the ability to speak it. This loss comes with a heavy price tag.

As evidenced by the following comments, for children who lived their earliest experiences in Spanish and who associate this language with the comfort of home, this loss brings a sense of melancholy and disconnection from the past, as well as loss of identity. Also, as evidenced in the following text, the loss of Spanish generally starts in the early years of school. The college years mark a reversal of this pattern. During this time, many college students from immigrant households actively seek to recover their lost skills as a way to find their identity.

1. At a young age I realized I had to master the English language in order to be successful at school and any other future career I dreamed of. I started to ignore my native tongue. It wasn't until I came to college that I realized I was losing a part of me. I started to forget some of the Spanish language, and most importantly, my background.

2. The people in my life either spoke only Spanish or were bilingual with English. As I progressed through school, I felt like Spanish was becoming less important because my friends and classmates stopped speaking it. Spanish also became a thing of the past at home because although my parents spoke it occasionally, most of our communication was in English. It wasn't until college, that I heard Spanish spoken in an exclusive setting. It was then that I realized that Spanish was becoming extinct in my life. And if Spanish was becoming extinct . . . what was to become of me? There is a link between people who share a common language.

3. Spanish was always my first language growing up. My father taught me English, and I would speak English with many of my neighbors, but at school I would usually speak Spanish. It was not until the second grade that I realized that I was supposed to speak English in school. I always thought our ESL workbooks were pretty easy, but I liked having time to talk to my friends, so I never told my teacher that I already knew how to speak English well. However my teacher realized it and he decided I should be put into a regular English class. I was distraught about this! I would cry and beg my mother to tell my teacher I didn't know how to speak English. I wanted to speak Spanish and only Spanish. This class was hard for me because I was not allowed to speak

Spanish any more. From what I recall, I would only be allowed one hour a day to speak Spanish with our teacher's aide. This was precious time for me. After third grade, I remember never having another teacher who could speak Spanish, which forced me to speak English all the time. I do remember speaking it at home, but it became less and less common over time. Second grade was the last time I considered myself a true Spanish speaker.

For children whose parents or relatives do not speak English or don't speak it well, the loss of Spanish radically alters family dynamics for the worse by rendering communication impossible or very difficult.

1. Spanish has always been in my life. When I was born, I learned Spanish first, from my Guatemalan parents. Once I started school I remember not being able to talk to anyone because I did not know English. That didn't last long. I quickly learned English, but I lost Spanish. This made it a struggle for me growing up. I can still remember not being able to talk to my grandparents or my family in Guatemala. I have come a long way since then though. Now I can speak both languages, though I still have some difficulty speaking Spanish, not because I cannot express myself but because I have an accent. I am still intimidated to talk to my family. For the most part, here in the U.S. it doesn't bother me. It does get to me when I go visit my family in Guatemala.

2. My parents didn't try too hard to teach us Spanish and my grandparents expressed disappointment to us that we couldn't speak to them in Spanish.

3. The way I got out of ESL was by speaking English all the way. I would always speak English at school, home, and everywhere else. Even my parents learned to speak English better. I started to speak only English to them and I regret it. The reason I regret is because when I went to El Salvador years ago, I couldn't have a real conversation with my relatives.

The loss of Spanish also exposes Latinos to the criticism and ridicule of other Latinos. Flipping the script of "the burden of being un-American for speaking Spanish," Latino children who don't speak Spanish face critiques of inauthenticity.

1. My boyfriend is Mexican but he doesn't speak Spanish. This bothers me because he can't communicate with my parents. One time, my

grandmother tried to talk to him, but he couldn't reply. I've always been embarrassed about my Spanish, but at least I can speak it, not like my boyfriend. My parents have told me that being Mexican or Mexican-American, we should speak Spanish without shame or embarrassment.

2. I am the only one of my group of friends that speaks fluent Spanish. I knew many girls in my school whose parents spoke Spanish, but they didn't. I think it was because they chose not to speak it. Most are "white washed" or *pochos.*

3. My high school was just minutes away from the U.S.-Mexican border. We had a lot of preppy kids who spoke Spanish really well. For them, a kid like me who did not know Spanish was a disgrace.

4. When I was little, I used to hang around kids of all races. At the time, I didn't know Spanish, but many people thought I did because of my looks. Kids would come up to me and start speaking Spanish and I would just look at them and say "Sorry, I don't speak Spanish." Then, they would look at me with this disgusting facial expression that would crumble any person to lost pieces of identity. I pushed myself hard to learn the language. But then, I struggled with being made fun of for speaking Spanish in a broken way. To this day, I still get ridiculed for the way I speak Spanish, and sometimes English, but I don't see the errors. I feel like I don't belong anywhere, not among my own race or any other.

Captured in the last comment is one of the greatest ironies surrounding the use of Spanish in the United States: Latino children who try to overcome the burden of not knowing Spanish by trying to learn it run up against another burden, namely, that of never being good enough. Chapter 1 offered a glimpse of this burden in the discussion surrounding the treatment of Spanish in school. The next section offers a more in-depth view of this phenomenon.

THE BURDEN OF NEVER BEING GOOD ENOUGH IN SPANISH

The fact that U.S. Latino children are not as fluent in Spanish as their peers in the Spanish-speaking world is not surprising. Raised in this country and schooled in English, their exposure to Spanish is quite limited. Despite this, they are expected to speak it well, if not to perfection, and are subjected to harsh condemnation for their mistakes, however small.

1. Since childhood I was never able to speak perfect Spanish. My mother used to speak English and Spanish, but my father only speaks Spanish and would speak to us in Spanish. I was never able to speak Spanish well. I also had problems understanding Spanish. In school I never had the need to speak Spanish, only when I was with my friends. Now that I am in college and am working, I realize the importance of speaking Spanish.

2. I can recall times when other Latinos have made fun of me for not speaking perfect Spanish. I felt bad but never paid much attention to it. Now I feel I have to practice Spanish more because I realize it's important for my job and to be able to communicate to my family.

3. Every year my family and I go to Mexico to visit our relatives. It's a great experience but some people have problems with the *norteños,* Northerners. Sometimes when I'm with my cousins and her friends and I say a word wrong, they laugh at me. I don't get angry, I just ask them how to say it correctly. But I have seen other people react very differently. They get angry or snap at those who make fun of them. This gives Mexicans the impression that Mexican-Americans are cranky, arrogant, or that they don't care about their roots. That may be the case for some of us, but it's not right to make fun of us because we make mistakes.

4. My grandmother gives my mom and my aunts a very hard time because they didn't teach us (i.e. the grandchildren) to speak perfect Spanish. It's very intimidating. None of us wants to mess up in Spanish when we speak with grandma.

5. I am proud of being a bilingual Latina in the United States. But it is hard to live up to the expectations of others when it comes to speaking, writing and understanding proper Spanish.

6. The first time I went to Mexico it was very difficult for me. My Spanish was not very good. I did everything possible to talk to my cousins but they made fun of me for not speaking it perfectly. They spent much of their time correcting me. At first it didn't bother me, but then I started to feel really bad. I had been so excited to meet my cousins and all they could do was make fun of me. That trip happened a long time ago when I was very young. Now my Spanish is much better, but I'm still feeling the effects. I'm shy about speaking Spanish. I know that there are plenty of people that speak Spanish better than me and there are others who

don't speak it very well. I just need to develop more confidence. I hope that my Spanish will continue to improve.

Overwhelmed by the burden of never being good enough in Spanish, some children become their own worst critics, to the point of silencing themselves.

A while ago, I offered to pair up with another student to give a tour of my university to Spanish-speaking parents. As soon as I started the tour, I felt extreme shame for not being able to speak fluently. I felt as though they looked at me as a disgrace for being Latina and not speaking Spanish. When I spoke, I could not think of certain words or I would use the wrong conjugation of verbs. As the tour went on, I spoke less and less, until I said nothing at all to save myself the terrible embarrassment. A couple of mothers had questions for me. I wish they hadn't asked—not because I didn't want to help them, but because I was incapable of being any help.

Taken together, the burden of being un-American, antisocial, or unintelligent for speaking Spanish and the burden of not knowing Spanish speak to one of the most vexing linguistic contradictions that U.S. Latinos have to contend with: paying a hefty price both for speaking and for not speaking Spanish.

THE BURDEN OF FALLING IN-BETWEEN LANGUAGES

Closely connected to the burden of never being good enough in Spanish is the burden of falling in-between languages. The sense of being alingual—that is, feeling inadequate in both English and Spanish—haunts many U.S. Latinos. Some of the background issues behind this burden are as follows:

1. As a Hispanic student in higher education, I feel that I'm at a slight disadvantage because my English isn't grand and my Spanish is far from perfect. I'm in the middle of two languages. Through the eyes of my family my English is great and my Spanish is completely broken. At the university I feel as if my English skills are so-so and according to the Spanish department my skills are considered native, which my family would never consider. It is strange how my ability to speak each language is analyzed differently by two diverse sides of my life.

2. I don't just have one language, but two. The first is Spanish—the language of my childhood and of my essence. The second is English—the language I had to learn to study and progress in this country. My English will never be perfect like that of an American and my accent will never go away. Some people have no idea of how difficult it can be to learn another language. There are so many memories that I would like forget, like the time a teacher told me that if I didn't speak English I had no business being in school. I felt so bad that I didn't want to go back to school.

To a large extent, the feeling of falling in-between languages—that is, of never being good enough in either—is rooted in the belief that true bilingualism entails having native-like ability in two languages. This common misconception defies reality and sets Latino youth up for disappointment, for the reasons explained by Stanford University professor Guadalupe Valdés:

> While absolutely equivalent abilities in two languages are theoretically possible, individuals seldom have access to two languages in exactly the same contexts in every domain of interaction. Neither do they have opportunities to use two languages to carry out the exact same functions with every person with whom they interact. Thus, they do not develop identical strengths in both languages.[42]

Latinos' linguistic insecurities also stem from the low regard that society has for the type of bilingualism they exemplify. Known as circumstantial bilingualism, this type of bilingualism is characteristic of individuals who come to learn a second language by virtue of their life circumstances, as is the case, for instance, with immigrants. Circumstantial bilingualism contrasts with elective bilingualism, which is characteristic of individuals who choose to learn a second language, typically, by enrolling in a class. Elective bilingualism is sometimes referred to as "elite bilingualism" because it is associated with higher socioeconomic status learners.

Though circumstantial bilinguals often attain high levels of proficiency, their language skills are often the target of criticism. The opposite is true of elective bilinguals: their skills are usually appreciated, regardless of how limited. Issues of prestige and power bear much to do with this state of affairs, as explained by sociolinguists: "Many Americans have long been of the opinion that bilingualism is a 'good thing' if it was acquired via travel (preferably to Paris) or via formal education (preferably at Harvard) but that is a 'bad thing' if it was acquired from one's immigrant parents or grandparents."[43]

All circumstantial bilinguals, the following students, are very critical of their linguistic abilities in English and Spanish. No doubt, the severe criticism that they have been subjected to in school (as discussed in Chapter 1) and other places has something to do with this. But the myth of equivalent—and native-like—abilities in two languages and the low status of circumstantial bilingualism also play a significant role.

1. It seems that the more English I learn, the more Spanish I forget. That is a problem because a lot of times I am looked down upon when I cannot hold a conversation in Spanish. Not knowing English or Spanish makes Latino students feel like they're outsiders like they don't belong.

2. Sometimes it is hard to go back and forth between languages. To speak proper English/Spanish can be very hard sometimes. At school all my friends speak proper English and no Spanish, but at home my family and I speak Spanish, though not proper.

3. My parents are from Mexico and they like to travel at least once a year there. My two siblings and I are all bilingual but going to a country that speaks only Spanish may be hard sometimes. Every year when we travel to Mexico we have a hard time communicating in Spanish. My siblings and I fluently speak Spanish but sometimes we feel more comfortable speaking in English. If any of our family members hear us speak English they give us a look that seems to say "don't speak that language." Every time we go to Mexico we try not to speak English at all. Sometimes my brothers and I feel like if we're here in the U.S we have to speak perfect English, but then if were in Mexico we have to speak perfect Spanish. However, this becomes very difficult if at school you only speak English and almost no Spanish. I think that this shows that it may not only affect the U.S but sometimes it can affect part of the culture itself.

Latinos speak different types of English. Foreign-born Latinos speak a nonnative version of English, typically with an accent. However, the presence of a foreign accent in such speakers is not necessarily an indicator of poor command of English. Indeed, there are many individuals with a strong command of English grammar and a large vocabulary, who also have a noticeable foreign accent. So common is this phenomenon that linguists actually have a name for it: the "Henry Kissinger Effect," coined after President Nixon's secretary of state, whose command of English is superb, despite having a very pronounced German accent.

Many U.S.-born Latinos speak standard English, the English used in schools and professional circles. Others speak a native version of English, which is considered nonstandard because of the influence of Spanish or of African American Vernacular English, commonly known as "Ebonics."[44] As we saw in Chapter 1, being labeled a speaker of a nonstandard variety of English can rob children of important academic, social, and ultimately professional opportunities.

The same is true for children who speak a nonstandard variety of Spanish, especially when that variety is Spanglish, the focus of the next burden.

THE BURDEN OF BEING LINGUISTIC *MESTIZOS*

This section derives its name from a quote by Chicana writer, Gloria Anzaldúa, which appears later in this section. In Spanish, the word *mestizo* refers to a person of mixed blood, typically of Indian and European extraction. In this discussion, we use the word in reference to the mixing of languages.

Some of the harshest linguistic criticism directed at U.S. Latinos concerns their use of English words and phrases when speaking Spanish. The term "Spanglish" is sometimes used derisively in reference to this practice. Such criticism obscures the fact that most U.S. Spanish varieties are highly intelligible to Spanish speakers abroad and that language mixing, or code-switching, as it is called in linguistics, is a common phenomenon when two or more languages coexist in close proximity. (See Table 2.4.)

Table 2.4   Commonly used Spanglish words

English	Spanish	Spanglish
Market	*Mercado*	marqueta
Lunch	*Almuerzo*	lonche
Truck	*Camión*	troca
Nurse	*Enfermera*	norsa
Yard	*patio, jardín*	yarda

But Spanglish is more than just a grab bag of words. It is a rule-governed code that fulfills the communicative needs of its speakers. To many U.S. Latinos, it is also a marker of identity, a hybrid code that captures their essence better than any single language. In a prizewinning essay, former UC Davis student, Rosa María Jiménez, explains the significance of Spanglish for Chicanos.

> Spanglish is culturally significant because it reflects our identity. Culture consists of customs, traditions, food, clothing, music, art, and language. In the same way that Spanglish unites the strengths of the English and Spanish languages, so too are Chicanos a union of the American and Mexican cultures. Code-switching not only reflects our identity, but also provides a means for us to strengthen each other. By speaking Spanglish, we restore pride in our language and in ourselves. If my friend says, "*Rosa, hay que irnos a la fiesta temprano* because it's Cinco de Mayo and there's going to be a lot of people," I feel a deeper cultural link with her than if she simply says, "Rosa, let's go early to the party because it's Cinco de Mayo and there's going to be a lot of people. . . . As Chicanos, we have our distinct language and culture which help us to seek equal access, opportunity, and justice without being absorbed by mainstream society. Spanglish allows us to communicate in a language that reflects the complexities of the Chicano identity. It is an innovative language that defines, unites and empowers the Chicano Community. "*¡Qué Viva* the Spanglish language!"[45]

The following comment offers a more unusual use of Spanglish, namely, as a clever strategy for countering the burden of being un-American, anti-social, or unintelligent for speaking Spanish in public.

> In first grade, two kids were speaking Spanish making fun of another student. That student told the teacher and she wasn't too happy. She told us how wrong it was to make fun of others and implied that we shouldn't be speaking Spanish because we could be misinterpreted. Thereafter, whenever I spoke Spanish I felt that other could think that I was talking badly about them. Even now, if I am talking to a girlfriend in Spanish and a person who doesn't look Hispanic is around I tend to switch to Spanglish. This way, I don't entirely leave Spanish, but I also leave no room for misinterpretations. I would say that at a young age I was molded by my experiences to think about

speaking Spanish exclusively for home and with private conversations with close friends.

However, not all U.S. Latinos embrace the symbolic importance of Spanglish or recognize its tactical value. One particularly vocal critic of Spanglish is Professor Roberto González Echevarría of Yale University. The following excerpt is from an editorial he wrote for the *New York Times*. Recalling Dame Edna's comment about the help, the first line bears the telltale signs of linguistic criticism that is rooted in disapproval of its speakers. Subsequent lines betray a similar sentiment:

> The sad reality is that Spanglish is primarily the language of poor Hispanics, many barely literate in either language. They incorporate English words and constructions into their daily speech because they lack the vocabulary and education in Spanish to adapt to the changing culture around them. Educated Hispanics who do likewise have a different motivation: Some are embarrassed by their background and feel empowered by using English words and directly translated English idioms. Doing so, they think, is to claim membership in the mainstream. Politically, however, Spanglish is a capitulation; it indicates marginalization, not enfranchisement.[46]

Criticisms of Spanglish strike particularly close to Latinos' heart. Chicana writer Gloria Anzaldúa likens this criticism to being culturally crucified: "*Somos los del espanol deficiente.* We are your linguistic nightmare, your linguistic aberration, your linguistic *mestizaje,*[47] the subject of your *burla.* Because we speak with tongues of fire we are culturally crucified. Racially, culturally and linguistically *somos huerfanos*—we speak an orphan tongue."[48]

Like many U.S. Latinos, our students are of two minds about Spanglish. On the one hand, they embrace it as a marker as their hybrid identity, much like Rosa María Jiménez. At the same time, buying into the criticisms of people like Professor Echevarría, they berate themselves and others for using it. The third entry in the following text makes clever use of Spanglish to express this ambivalence. At the end of this chapter, we feature another piece in Spanglish, the context of discussing the upside of bilingualism.

1. It's not that I do it on purpose, nor that I do it to deny our language, but Spanish has always been difficult for me. I start my conversation

in Spanish, but somehow I always end up finishing it in English. My thoughts have always been better said in English rather than Spanish. It's like nobody understands what I'm saying when I say it in Spanish. My sister is constantly asking me why I respond in English when I am spoken to in Spanish. My response—'I don't do it on purpose!' Growing up as a kid, my family always told me that speaking two languages is better than one, but what do you do when one language is better understood than another? Of course I speak Spanish and I understand it sometimes, but I believe my primary language is Spanglish.

2. For me, speaking two languages is both good and bad. It's good because I can speak with Spanish-speaking people and I can speak with English-speaking people. It's bad because I confuse the languages sometimes. I am most comfortable with Spanglish.

3. Dear World:

Being bilingual and living en Los Estados Unidos is not very easy. Having double vocabulary es difficult porque sometimes you get so frustrated that you don't know if to say your words in English or español. Spanglish—that's what I know how to speak—lo que sé hablar. A muchos les molesta (many are bothered) that I mix my two languages pero they don't understand que being Latina means hablar dos lenguas. Latina soy y Spanglish is what I speak.

W.Z.

THE BURDEN OF BEING GOOD ENOUGH IN TWO LANGUAGES

The flip side of the burden of falling in-between languages is the burden of being good enough in two languages. Children who are proficient Spanish–English bilinguals are often called upon to translate for adults, especially, teachers and family members. In many cases, translating, or language brokering, can be a very satisfying and enriching experience for children. However, translating can also create anxiety, shame, and insecurity in children. The root of this problem is that bilingual children are often asked to act as translators, without the consideration of whether they have the emotional or cognitive maturity required for the task. As a result, being good enough in two languages can land children in highly distressing situations.

Complicated high-stakes tasks, such as business transactions or delicate legal situations, can create undue stress for children and put unreasonable demands on them.

1. Being a young lad I would always have to translate for my mom. She would give me documents about immigration that sometimes I just couldn't translate for I didn't know what those words meant. I would try my best but I simply couldn't translate the vocabulary in those letters. I was only around eight years old and it was really hard. At times my mom would get angry at me. I didn't understand why she would be upset, but I guess the frustration of her not knowing and me not being able to translate was frustrating for us both.

2. You can imagine what weight I was carrying throughout my adolescence having to translate for my parents. At times I would get so frustrated that my own dad would expect so much from me at my age. But at other times I would get mad at myself for not being able to translate words like "escrow" or words that I had never seen in my short life.

3. A large portion of the paperwork my father had to fill out to refinance the house was too complicated for him to understand since his ability to read English is very limited. I remember attempting to read the paperwork and there were many words that I could not understand myself since I was only 11 years old. I remember my father getting frustrated and angry at me, telling me that since I knew English and had been studying it in school for a couple of years, I should be able to comprehend what was written. I had to explain to my father that I was just a child and that I had a lot to learn. I felt angry that my father would expect so much of me and yet I also felt disappointed because I let him down.

Translating at the doctor's office can thrust children into adult conversations, making them feel embarrassed.

When I was in high school I had to go to the doctor with my aunt to help translate for her. I was the only one who could go because everyone else was busy. When we got to the office we checked in, but when they called my aunt in for her exam, they didn't want me to go with her because I was a minor. I had no idea what the appointment was for, but they let me go in with her when I explained I was translating for my aunt since the bilingual nurse was unavailable. It turns out they started examining her breasts but I was embarrassed to be talking about such things. The doctor started asking me to translate questions and some of them were about things I never wanted to know about; such as her sexual relationship with my uncle. When my aunt gave her responses I turned red and felt even more embarrassed that I had to repeat them to the doctor. I was so embarrassed that after that I was not able to bring myself to see my aunt or uncle for some time.

Translating in school can pit children against their peers or put them in the difficult situation of having to convey unpleasant news to adults.

1. I remember my third grade teacher asking me to help her during a parent meeting. The parent turned out to be my best friend's mother! My friend was in trouble for not doing his homework. I felt that I was getting him in trouble with his mom because I was translating for the teacher. My friend did not speak to me for two weeks after that.

2. Often when other students would misbehave, the teacher would ask me to call their parents and let them know how their child was behaving. Many parents didn't like to receive bad news about their kids and they would yell at me, when I was only the translator. They would say rude things about the teacher, but of course, I didn't translate that back to him.

3. As a Spanish-speaking child in high school I was often called upon by the teacher to translate. Many parents would become upset because I was the one calling and not the teacher. The frustration of not being able to communicate to parents was too much for him. He asked me to teach him some basic words to communicate with parents and I agreed because I was tired of getting yelled at.

Translating for one's parents at parent–teacher conferences presents its own set of challenges. Communicating positive results can prove awkward and rob children of some of the enjoyment of the moment. Communicating negative news can be distressing and humiliating.

1. When I was in elementary school I was always used as a translator. When my parents had to attend a meeting with the teachers to talk about how I was doing and my grades, I would be there as a translator. Although I was helping my parents communicate with the teachers, I really didn't like it. I would always do my best in school, but I just think it would have been more exciting and believable if my parents would have it heard from the teachers. I think my parents would have felt more proud of me if they would have heard from another adult about what a good student I was.

2. I had to translate for my parents as well as I could, the fact I was not doing well in school because my English wasn't very good. Not only

did I have to hear from my teacher that I needed much improvement, but I had to tell my parents the horrible news.

THE BEAUTY OF THIS COUNTRY IN TWO LANGUAGES

With all of the burdens associated with living under the shadow of two languages, why would anyone want to recover or develop their Spanish, let alone use it?

The comments featured in this section resonate with the following reasons offered by researchers: "Individuals that are fluently bilingual can move effectively between their home and host country cultures. Moreover retaining fluency in one's home language allows enduring access to resources engrained within extended family and ethnic community contexts. This may be particularly important for youth as sharing a common language with parents guarantee that children are not completely alienated from their families of origin and that parental authority is maintained."[49]

Though not addressed by our students, there are cognitive benefits to individuals, as well as competitive advantages to U.S. society associated with bilingualism that should be recognized in the context of this discussion. In the cognitive arena, benefits include increased gray matter in the areas of the brain involved in fluency and auditory processing of language, better performance in tests of executive function, including problem solving, mental flexibility, control of attention, and greater cognitive reserve in the elderly, possibly delaying the onset of Alzheimer's disease.[50] In terms of advantages to society, Secretary of Education Arne Duncan notes: "To prosper economically and to improve relations with other countries, Americans need to read, speak and understand other languages."[51]

Also focused on this country, the following student speaks of the beauty of this country in two languages.

One day at work a little old lady came up to me and asked why we advertised in Spanish. This was the U.S., she said, and we should only speak English. I felt angry but I couldn't say anything. Later I felt bad for her because she has never experienced the beauty of this country in two languages.

What is this experience like? Our students single out three particularly rewarding and meaningful experiences associated with bilingualism: (1) being able to help those in need, (2) pushing the boundaries of expression, and (3) benefiting from the cultural capital of Latino families and communities. We address the first two in this final section of this chapter, taking up the remaining one in Chapters 3 and 4.

HELPING THOSE IN NEED

As we saw in Chapter 1, Latino youth who overcome obstacles are committed to helping others do the same. The students in the following text describe some of the ways in which their bilingualism contributes to that end.

Remarkably, at the center of all of these situations is an act of translation. Contradicting earlier depictions of translation, these students describe feeling good, proud, and honored by the opportunity to help others. Rather than feeling anxious, embarrassed, or insecure, they convey a sense of accomplishment and fellowship.

How can this be? We believe that one reason is that they involve situations that are cognitively, emotionally, and linguistically appropriate for the children. In other words, the tasks are within their range of competency and maturity. Another reason is that the children are allowed to exercise agency with regard to their use of language. For example, in some cases, they translate out of their own choice, and in others, they exercise their own judgment about what to translate and how to do it. Quite likely, this has the effect of empowering children.

The tasks span a range of contexts and levels of difficulty. Crucially, they are not all easy tasks, and they are not all low-stakes tasks. What makes them manageable and rewarding is that they are within the grasp and choice of the youth.

Translating in School

1. Every couple of months, my high school would have a "peer court," where students would determine the punishment of their peers that had done minor crimes. The "accused" would stand in front of their parents and the peer judges and talk about what they had done. On one occasion, the person who translated for parents who didn't speak English couldn't make it and the teacher asked me to fill in for her. I immediately accepted—I love the idea of helping out. The day came and I was introduced to the parent I would be translating for. I was a bit nervous and didn't want to say the wrong things. I saw the woman's face and felt her shame and fear. She had been through one of these situations before. When it was their turn to go on stage, my insides felt like they were going to drop. It turned out that the student had tried to spend

a fake $100 bill and was caught. My Spanish helped me console the mother and to give her a voice and some dignity before the group. When it was over, I realized how much I had been able to help this family out because I knew Spanish. I was proud to be able to help, although I felt very sad for them.

2. When the school nurse saw me pass by the office at my elementary school, she immediately stopped me and asked for my help. She told me she has been waiting for the secretary to translate an emergency form that was written in Spanish. The nurse said she was frustrated for she was constantly asking for help and not getting any. She gave me the form to translate, it was only 3 sentences. The nurse thanked me so much that it made me proud of who I am. I hadn't felt like my Spanish was useful because I always speak it at home, but for someone who knows nothing it is a great help. I also felt good about myself and it made me want to continue my Spanish skills to a more professional level.

3. By the time I was in junior high and high school I began volunteering for teachers to translate during their meetings with parents whose knowledge of the English language was limited. This inspired other students at my school to do the same. It felt great to be able to help so many people get involved in their child's education. I was recognized for the work I had done during my school Senior Awards. I felt really honored.

4. I recall an incident in high school where I translated for one of my teachers at a Back-To-School night. Some of the parents didn't speak English and the teacher didn't speak Spanish so he was stuck in a difficult position. I stepped in and cleared things up.

Translating at Work

1. I have a part-time job as a cashier in a local mall and I am the only one who speaks Spanish. Whenever there's a customer who speaks only Spanish, they come to me asking for help. The customers are always pleased when they have been helped by someone who speaks their language.

2. At work, my boss always asks me to translate for him when he's talking to our busboys and dishwashers. I always notice that my Spanish-speaking customers always seem more comfortable when they know I speak Spanish. It seems like there is a better connection between us.

3. When I was 14 years old I worked for a veterinarian. I always had to translate because none of the clients spoke English and nobody else in

the office spoke Spanish. I grew from this experience because I learned a lot and I like helping people.

4. I remember a lady came in to the doctor's office where I worked to prepare for an upcoming surgery. The lady was agreeing to everything even though she didn't know what the doctor was telling. Finally, the doctor noticed she didn't understand and she came to see if anyone knew Spanish and I said I did. Later on, the doctor gave me a raise because he said it was good that I helped and he realized knowing different languages really helps out.

Translating for Parents

I am the child of immigrants from Central and South America. Both of my parents are college graduates from their respective countries and immigrated here for political reasons and the opportunity of attaining a higher economic status. Growing up I consumed massive quantities of television, specifically PBS, and through PBS I effectively acquired and expanded my English. So, after a day at school of reading, writing and speaking English I would go home and "practice" by viewing PBS, since my parents did not speak English. Ultimately, I became very limited with my Spanish but excelled in English; this consistently frustrated my parents who felt a disconnect between them and me. Not until my mother decided to open her own business did my Spanish expand. My mother knew little English at that time and at the age of 9 or 10 I became a translator for my mother in a business setting. I remember speaking for her at City Hall, with property managers, with banks and writing letters for her clients. The necessity of being able to communicate legal and business documents to my mom pushed me to expand my lexicon in Spanish.

Translating in the Community

I was once waiting for a bus and a stranger came up to me and asked me in Spanish if I spoke English. He needed help to speak with a supervisor. He asked me to say something to his supervisor over the phone. Usually, when people know that I'm bilingual they ask for my help.

Pushing the Boundaries of Expression

Bilingualism offers a rich palette of linguistic colors and textures that expand the expressive boundaries of U.S. Latinos beyond the confines of any single language. By way of illustration, we close this chapter with a poem written in Spanglish by a young Mexican American woman by the name of Carla González. A native of Los Angeles, California, and a recent graduate from California State University, Long Beach, Carla bears the distinction of being the first in her family to earn a college degree. Along the way, she encountered many of the burdens of bilingualism discussed in this chapter, including, as described in this poem, the burden of translating for others, the burden of never being good enough in Spanish, the burden of falling in-between languages, and the burden of Spanglish. Resisting the criticism of the voices of authority and the pressure to abandon Spanish, Carla challenges her critics to give her a better education and proudly claims Spanglish as her Latin gift. We have chosen not to translate the poem into English, as that would take away from the very point of using Spanglish.

My Latin Gift

by Carla González

Yes, soy American but también latina

Sé hablar English, español y Spanglish

Yes, teacher I can speak English sin hablar español

Oh, disculpe, I mean I'm sorry

¿Por qué no debo mezclar los dos idiomas?

Yes, soy bilingual y estoy proud

Aunque a veces es stressful y challenging

Yes, mom te puedo traducir para que hables con my teacher

Mom, I don't know como decirte lo que mi teacher te quiere decir

Yes, sé hablar English pero es difícil traducir, apenas soy una niña

Me estoy frustrando, I am scared

Ya no quiero traducir, me estoy equivocando

Maybe, no soy bilingual

No puedo hablar ni English ni Spanish

Yes, voy a school para aprender, pero todos mis teachers hablan English

Casi nadie es como yo

Yes, soy latina

Don't laugh porque no sé what that word means o porque la pronuncie funny

Is it a pecado ser latina?

Why so many críticas y risas?

Mejor help me, educate me, dáme una mejor educación

Yes, soy latina

My language, Spanglish es un don

Para que me entiendan, déjenme traducirle

My language, Spanglish is a gift

My Latin gift

DISCUSSION QUESTIONS

1. At the beginning of this chapter, we posed three questions: Aren't immigrant children better served by leaving their home language behind? Aren't we better off as a country with English as our only language? Why are today's immigrants not learning English? Based on what you have read in this chapter as well as what you may know from personal experience, answer one or two of these questions.

2. Consider Carla González's poem. What burdens of bilingualism are addressed? What elements of the beauty of bilingualism are discussed?

3. A recent article in *Latina* magazine features celebrities like Selena Gomez and Jessica Alba explaining why they want to learn or improve their Spanish and sharing their language-learning strategies.[52] What impact, if any, do you think these statements of support by high-profile individuals have on Latino children? In your opinion, are they likely to lessen the burdens of living under the shadow of two languages? What, if anything, can lessen such burdens?

4. Besides the linguistic burdens discussed in this chapter, are you aware of any other ones? What about the rewards of bilingualism? Are there others not discussed here?

5. As we have seen, judgments about languages—both positive and negative—are often predicated on socioeconomic factors and perceptions about the people who speak them. Can you find examples from other languages besides Spanish that exemplify this principle? What

are the high-prestige and low-prestige foreign languages in the United States? What social values or perceptions lie behind the status of these languages? What about English, what dialects are considered low prestige? How are their speakers viewed?

6. Throughout the history of the United States, many immigrant languages have disappeared within three generations. What are the languages and cultures in your family background? How many people in the United States speak this language nowadays? Do you wish your family had maintained this language?

ONLINE RESOURCES ON SPANISH

Center for Applied Linguistics (http://www.cal.org/)
A nonprofit private institution applying knowledge about language to issues of concern to educators, policymakers, and immigrant and refugee service providers.

Center for Multilingual and Multicultural Research (http://www.usc.edu/dept/education/CMMR/cmmrhomepage.html)
Center at the University of Southern California that facilitates the dissemination of information on multilingual education and other topics related to immigrant languages.

Diccionario de la lengua española (http://www.rae.es/rae.html)
Free online Spanish language dictionary published by the Spanish Royal Academy

El Instituto Cervantes (http://www.cervantes.es/)
An institute created by the Spanish government to assist with the promotion and teaching of the Spanish language and the diffusion of the culture of Spain and Hispanic America.

National Heritage Language Resource Center (http://www.international.ucla .edu/languages/nhlrc)
One of 15 language resource centers funded by the U.S. government. The mission of this center is to develop effective pedagogical approaches for teaching heritage languages to children who speak a language other than English at home.

Tomás Rivera Policy Institute (http://www.trpi.org/)
A think tank devoted to researching a wide range of issues surrounding U.S. Latinos, including bilingualism, immigration, education, civic participation, etc.

Nobel Prize Winners in Literature from the Spanish-Speaking World
2010, Mario Vargas Llosa, Peru
1990, Octavio Paz, Mexico
1989, Camilo José Cela, Spain
1982, Gabriel García Márquez, Colombia

1977, Vicente Aleixandre, Spain
1971, Pablo Neruda, Chile
1967, Miguel Angel Asturias, Guatemala
1956, Juan Ramón Jiménez, Spain
1945, Gabriela Mistral, Chile
1922, Jacinto Benavente, Spain
1904, José Echegaray y Eizaguirre, Spain

NOTES

1. Dame Edna, "Ask Dame Edna." *Vanity Fair,* February 2003:116.
2. "El Español: Una Lengua Viva." Instituto Cervantes, 2013. http://www.cer vantes.es/sobre_instituto_cervantes/prensa/2013/noticias/diae-resumen-datos-2013.htm.
3. Rosina Lippi-Green, *English with an Accent: Language, Ideology, and Discrimination in the United States.* London & New York: Routledge, 1997.
4. Ilan Stavans, *On Borrowed Words: A Memoir of Language.* New York: Viking/Penguin, 2001.
5. Lippi-Green, *English with an Accent.*
6. "Languages of the World." Ethnologue, n.d. http://www.ethnologue.com/web.asp.
7. U.S. Census Bureau. http://www.Census.gov.
8. Maria Carreira, "Evaluating Spanish-language Vitality in the United States from a Capacity, Opportunity and Desire Framework." *Heritage Language Journal* 10, no. 3 (2014).
9. Ibid.
10. Ibid.
11. Ibid.
12. Ethnologue. "Languages of the World." http://www.ethnologue.com/web.asp.
13. In all but five of the countries in Table 2.1, Spanish is the de jure official language, meaning that it has official status by legislation. In Mexico, Argentina, Chile, Nicaragua, and Uruguay, Spanish does not have such status, but it functions as the de facto official language, meaning that it is the main language of communication and the language of official documents and schooling. Spanish had official status in the Philippines until 1973.
14. "The Numbers of Spanish Speakers in the World Exceeds 500 Million." *Spanish Language Domains,* July 26, 2012. http://www.spanishlanguagedo mains.com/the-numbers-of-spanish-speakers-in-the-world-exceeds-500-million/.
15. "Católogo de Las Lenguas Indígenas Nacionales." *Instituto Nacional de Lenguas Indigenas,* n.d. http://inali.gob.mx/.
16. David Graddol, *The Future of English?* London: The British Council, 2000.
17. Cathy Booth, "Miami: The Capital of Latin America." *Time,* June 24, 2001. http://www.time.com/time/magazine/article/0,9171,1101931202-162806,00.html.

18. Christine U. Grosse, "The Competitive Advantage of Foreign Languages and Cultural Knowledge." *Modern Language* 88, no. 3 (2004): 351–73.

19. Maria Carreria, "Professional Opportunities for Heritage Language Speakers." In *Handbook of Heritage, Community, and Native American Languages in the United States,* edited by T. Wiley, J. Kreeft Peyton, D. Christian, S. Moore, and N. Liu, 66–76. New York: Routledge and Center for Applied Linguistics, 2014.

20. Nelly Furmin, David Goldberg, and Natalia Lusin, *Enrollments in Languages Other Than English in United States Institutions of Higher Education.* Modern Language Association Web Publication. Modern Language Association, Autumn 2009.

21. Ana González-Barrera and Mark Hugo López, "Spanish Is the Most Spoken Non-English Language in U.S. Homes, Even among Non-Hispanics." *Pew Hispanic Center,* August 13, 2013. http://www.pewresearch.org/fact-tank/2013/08/13/spanish-is-the-most-spoken-non-english-language-in-u-s-homes-even-among-non-hispanics/.

22. This quote comes from a letter by Thomas Jefferson to his nephew, Peter Carr. The Writings of Thomas Jefferson, (1904) p. 44. Thomas Jefferson Memorial Association of America.

23. Ofelia García and Leah Mason, "Where in the World Is U.S. Spanish? Creating a Space of Opportunity for U.S. Latinos." In *Language and Poverty,* edited by W. Harbort, S. Wayne, A. McConnell-Ginet, Amanda Miller, and J. Whitmann, 78–101. Bristol: Multilingual Matters, 2009.

24. David Weber, *The Spanish Frontier in North America.* New Haven, CT: Yale University Press, 1992.

25. Camille Ryan, "American Community Survey—22." *U.S. Census Bureau,* 2013. http://www.census.gov.

26. Ethnologue. "Languages of the World." http://www.ethnologue.com/web.asp.

27. Michele Serros, "Michele Serros: Latino Themed Writing 101." *Fox News Latino,* January 27, 2012. http://latino.foxnews.com/latino/entertainment/2012/01/27/michele-serros-latino-themed-writing-101/#ixzz1lAYJjqn7.

28. "Dallas Police Gave Tickets for Not Speaking English." *Yahoo! News,* October 23, 2009. http://news.yahoo.com/s/afp/20091023/ts_alt_afp/uscrimeracism_20091023230854.

29. Sam Verhovek, "Mother Scolded by Judge for Speaking in Spanish." *New York Times,* August 30, 1995. http://www.nytimes.com/1995/08/30/us/mother-scolded-by-judge-for-speaking-in-spanish.html.

30. Anne Ryman and Ofelia Madrid, "State Investigating Teacher Accused of Hitting Students." *The Arizona Republic,* January 16, 2004. http://azbilingualed.org/AABE%20Site/AABE--News%202004/state_investigating_teacher_accu.htm.

31. "The GOP: Se Habla Espanol?" *The Seoul Times,* n.d., sec. Art & Living. http://theseoultimes.com/ST/?url=/ST/db/read.php?idx=130.

32. Catherine Valenti, "English-Only Work Rules on the Rise." *Hire Diversity,* December 1, 2013. http://www.hirediversity.com/news/newsbyid.asp?id=14020.

33. Phillip Carter, "National Narratives, Institutional Ideologies and Local Talk: The Discoursive Production of Spanish in a 'New' U.S. Latino Community." *Language in Society* 43 (2014): 209–240.

34. Shirin Hakimzadeh and D'Vera Cohn, "English Usage among Hispanics in the United States." *Pew Hispanic Center,* November 29, 2007. http://www.pewhispanic.org/2007/11/29/english-usage-among-hispanics-in-the-united-states/.

35. Lesley Bartlett and Ofelia García, *Additive Schooling in Subtractive Times. Dominican Immigrant Youth in the Heights.* Nashville, TN: Vanderbilt University Press, 2011.

36. "Truth Squad: Did Gingrich Refer to Spanish as 'gheto' Language? *CNN Wire Staff.* January 27, 2012. http://www.cnn.com/2012/01/27/politics/truth-squad-spanish/index.html.

37. Joshua A. Fishman, Vladimir Nahirny, John Hofman, and Robert Hayden, *Language Loyalty in the United States: The Maintenance and Perpetuation of Non-English Mother Tongues by American Ethnic and Religious Groups.* The Hague, the Netherlands: Mouton, 1996.

38. Robert Suro, "National Survey of Latinos. Pew Hispanic Center/Kaiser Family Foundation." *Pew Hispanic Center,* 2002. http://www.pewhispanic.org.

39. Calvin Veltman, "The American Linguistic Mosaic: Understanding Language Shift in the United States." In *New Immigrants in the United States: Background for Second Language Educators,* edited by S.L. McKay and S.C. Wong, 58–93. Cambridge: Cambridge University Press, 2000.

40. Chantilly Patiño, "Bicultural Identity: My Husband's Story of Life on 'La Frontera.'" *Bicultural Mom: Raising Niños in a Mixed & Matched World,* November 9, 2011. http://www.biculturalmom.com/2011/11/09/bicultural-living-my-husbands-story-of-life-on-la-frontera/.

41. Lippi-Green, *English with an Accent.*

42. Guadalupe Valdés, "Heritage Language Students: Profiles and Possibilities." In *Heritage Languages in America. Preserving a National Resource,* edited by J. Keeft Peyton, D. Ranard, and S. McGinnis, 40. McHenry, IL: Delta Systems, 2011.

43. Joshua A. Fishman, Vladimir Nahirny, John E. Hofman, and Robert, G. Hayden, *Language Loyalty in the United States: The Maintenance and Perpetuation of Non-English Mother Tongues by American Ethnic and Religious Groups. Language* 44, no. 1 (Mar., 1968): 198–201.

44. Following linguistic practice, we use the term "nonstandard" in reference to versions of English that do not conform to the norms of the language spoken by middle-class white American males. Though research has shown that these versions of English are as linguistically complex, rule-governed, and expressive as the standard language, they are frequently stigmatized for social reasons—namely, the low social standing of its speakers.

45. Rosa María Jiménez, "Spanglish: The Language of Chicanos," *Prized Writing: The Essay and Scientific & Technical Writing* no. 1995–1996 (n.d.). http://

prizedwriting.ucdavis.edu/past/1995-1996/201cspanglish201d-the-language-of-chicanos.

46. Roberto González Echevarría, *New York Times,* March 28, 1997. http://www.ampersandcom.com/GeorgeLeposky/spanglish.htm.

47. Derived from *mestizo, mestizaje* typically refers to mixing or blending of race. Here it refers to the mixing of languages.

48. Gloria Anzaldúa, *Borderlands: La Frontera. The New Mestiza.* San Francisco: Aunt Lute Books, 1999.

49. Cynthia García Coll, Flannery Patton, Amy Kerivan Marks, Radosveta Dimitrova, Rui Yang, Gloria A. Suarez, and Andrea Patrico, "Understanding the Immigrant Paradox in Youth: Developmental and Contextual Consideration." In *Realizing the Potential of Immigrant Youth,* edited by Ann S. Masten, Karmela Liebkind, and Donald J. Hernández. Cambridge: Cambridge University Press, 2012.

50. Albert Costa and Núria Sebastian-Galles, "How Does the Bilingual Experience Sculpt the Brain?" *Nature Reviews Neuroscience* 15 (2014): 336–45. http://www.sap.upf.edu/node/381.

51. David Skorton and Glenn Altschuler, "America's Foreign Language Deficit." *Forbes,* August 27, 2012. http://www.forbes.com/sites/collegeprose/2012/08/27/americas-oreign-language-deficit/.

52. Lee Hernández, "Exclusive: 9 Latino Celebs Who Are Learning Spanish." *Latina,* March 15, 2013.

THREE

Voces about Culture

*Learning about our culture and history is a way of learning about
ourselves, an acceptance of oneself as an individual and of her/his
people. Then we may educate the world, including our own communities about ourselves. But more importantly, it will show us another
way of seeing life and the world we live in now.*[1]

These words by writer Ana Castillo provide the impetus for this chapter, which is intended to serve as a primer on U.S. Latino culture. Some
of the customs, practices, and perspectives discussed here have their origins in one or more countries of the Spanish-speaking world, while others
respond to the experiences of Latinos in the United States and represent
new paths forged at the intersection of multiple languages and cultures.

The Spanish-speaking countries in the Americas share cultural traditions and values and beliefs by virtue of their historical ties to Spain. At
the same time, just as Americans, Australians and Canadians are different
from each other, so are Argentineans, Mexicans, and Cubans. National
differences between Latinos are too many and too complex to examine
here. Suffice it to say that they manifest themselves across many domains,
including food, music, traditions, sociopolitical history, and, as discussed
in Chapter 2, language.

Underscoring this diversity, Mexican writer Carlos Fuentes writes: "We
are in the first place a multiracial, policultural continent."[2] These words
take on added meaning in the United States, where the myriad cultural currents of the Spanish-speaking world and the United States come together.

The Borderlands, as writer Gloria Anzaldúa has baptized the territory at the intersection of these currents, is a place of bewildering ambiguities and colorful juxtapositions. She writes: "To live in the Borderlands means you are neither hispana india negra española ni gabachacha, eres mestiza, mulata, half-breed while carrying all five races on your back not knowing which side to turn to, or to run from. . . . To live in the Borderlands means to put chile in the borscht, eat whole wheat tortillas, speak Tex-Mex with a Brooklyn accent; be stopped by la migra at the border checkpoints."[3]

Our goal for this chapter is to draw a map of the Borderlands, delineating key historical and cultural currents that have shaped its present-day contours and highlighting points of interests and pathways of special significance to Latino youth. Against this backdrop, we examine the tools and resources deployed by Latino youth to navigate the ambiguities of the Borderlands, clear obstacles in their way, and open new spaces in the American landscape.

Our journey through the Borderlands starts with a poem by Analiese Camacho that addresses some of the issues that occupy us in this chapter—for example, identity, acculturation, and race—and captures the collage of colors, images, and sounds that make up the Borderlands.

Born and raised in Azusa, California, Analiese is a 2014 graduate of Azusa Pacific University with a bachelor of arts degree in English. As of the writing of this book, she is preparing to move to the Las Vegas Valley to teach high school English as a Teach for America corps member. She hopes to inspire young Latinos and Latinas to pursue higher education while always remembering their Hispanic upbringing.

Este Cuerpo

This body, believe it or not, hasn't always had brown pride running through its veins.

And I'm not going to lie—this body didn't always walk around thinking *¡Viva México!*

This body has not always desired to walk the same streets as *sus abuelos en Guadalajara*

because this body did not always know who or what it belonged to,

but it now knows that it belongs to *la historia de su familia.*

When I look in the mirror I see this body painted red.

Rojo como chiles, como menudo, como tomates.

I see green.

Verde como aguacates, como guacamole, como limón y cilantro.

I see white.

Blanco como arroz con leche como avena.

When I look in the mirror I see that this body is painted red, white, and green.

I am the colors of my flag.

Soy los colores de mi bandera.

This body understands that when other people look at it they only see the color brown.

Color café como frijoles como el mole de mi abuela.

This body wishes other bodies were color blind so my body could be color blind

then we could all put color to the side and finally leave it there.

This body is not always sure whether to use *ser o estar, por o para.*

This body has never known how to correctly speak in the past tense

porque este cuerpo está demasiado ocupado viviendo lo presente.

This body has found its voice.

Este cuerpo ha encontrado su voz.

With its voice this body practices its *grito Mexicano.*

This body comes alive to the sounds of mariachis and bidi bidi bom bom.

This body answers to both its first language *y su segunda.*

This body may walk and talk the American way,

but it still daydreams of time spent across its neighbor's borders.

Este cuerpo es fuerte y duro.

Hermoso y elegante.

Educado y humano.

Este cuerpo es igual.

Este cuerpo es tratando y aprendiendo y viviendo.

Este cuerpo es Mexicano.

This body is strong and tough.

Beautiful and elegant.

Educated and human.

This body is equal.

This body is trying and learning and living.

This body is Mexican.

THE BORDERLANDS BY THE NUMBERS

Identity[4]

29: Percentage of U.S. Latinos who say they share a common culture with other U.S. Latinos

51: Percentage of U.S. Latinos who identify themselves first by their country of origin

24: Percentage of U.S. Latinos who describe themselves as "Hispanic" or "Latino(a)"

21: Percentage of U.S. Latinos who call themselves "American"

47: Percentage of Latinos who think of themselves as a typical American

47: Percentage of Latinos who think of themselves as very different from the typical American

51: Percentage of Latinos who identify their race as "some other race"

36: Percentage of Latinos who identify their race as white

3: Percentage of Latinos who identify their race as black

Religion[5]

68: Percentage of U.S. Latinos who are Catholic (*v.* 15% Evangelical and 8% secular)

35: Percentage of American Catholics who are Latino

15: Percentage of Latinos who are born-again or evangelical Protestants

8: Percentage of Latinos who do not identify with any religion

Civic Participation[6]

8.4: The percentage of voters in the 2012 presidential election who were Hispanic

1.2 million: The number of Latinos who are veterans of the U.S. Armed Forces

ORIGINS AND DESTINATIONS: THE CARDINAL POINTS IN THE BORDERLANDS

In raw numbers, Latino immigration exceeds that of any other group in this country's history. However, measured proportionally against the total U.S. population, Latino immigration rates are actually lower than those of the 19th century and the early 20th century, when many Europeans immigrated to this country. Spanish-speaking immigrants were brought here primarily by economic and political reasons. World War II brought a large influx of Mexican immigrants under the "Bracero" program.[7] The Cuban Revolution brought the first wave of Cuban refugees starting in 1959, followed by the "Marielitos" in the 1980s and the "Balseros" in the 1990s.[8] Central Americans arrived mostly in the latter part of the 20th century fleeing civil strife, wars, and natural disasters. Many Salvadorians, Hondurans, and Nicaraguans arrived with Temporary Protected Status, which is granted by the U.S. government to individuals fleeing unsafe circumstances in their home countries.

Nearly two-thirds of U.S. Latinos (65%) trace their origins to Mexico. Puerto Ricans are the second largest Latino population, at 9.4 percent, followed by Salvadorians at 3.8 percent, Cubans at 3.6 percent, Dominicans at 3.0 percent, and 2.3percent Guatemalan.[9] Contrary to popular perception, the overwhelming majority of Latinos—about 83 percent—are in this country legally. Because Puerto Rico is a U.S. territory, all Puerto Ricans are citizens of the United States, and therefore have legal status, though they cannot run for U.S. president or vote in presidential elections. However, Puerto Rican delegates vote at the national conventions of both major parties, which is the reason why the island holds presidential primaries.

Latinos in the United States have different settlement patterns, depending on their country of origin. The majority of Mexican Americans live in the Southwest, particularly in California, Texas, and New Mexico. Puerto Ricans and Dominicans are concentrated in the Northeast, primarily in New York, New Jersey, and Eastern Pennsylvania. Many Cubans have settled in Florida, while South Americans have concentrated on the East Coast and Central Americans on the West Coast. Recently, Latino immigration has spread to nontraditional destinations such as Alabama, South Carolina, Tennessee, Kentucky, and South Dakota, which bear the distinction of being the fastest-growing Hispanic states in the first decade of the 21st century. However, even as Latino immigration is spreading to new areas, it remains geographically concentrated. More than half (55%) of U.S. Latinos reside in just three states: California, Texas, and Florida.[10]

In the United States, national differences between Latinos tend to be blurred, usually for reasons of expediency and sometimes ignorance. For example, in places where the majority of the Latino population is of Mexican origin, all Latinos are often assumed to be Mexican, or, if not, they are expected to be familiar enough with Mexican culture to answer questions surrounding its cuisine, history, traditions, and so on. This is akin to expecting an American to know the ins and outs of Australian culture, by virtue of the fact that both speak English.

Another misconception—that all people from the Spanish-speaking world fit a certain look—leads to misplaced assumptions about those who don't conform to that look. An amusing incident involving two Cubans in Chicago, one of Chinese descent and the other of Spanish descent (author Maria Carreira's father), illustrates this point. Running into each other in an elevator, the two men exchanged pleasantries in rapid Spanish. After the Cuban Chinese man left the elevator, a non-Spanish-speaking acquaintance of Mr. Carreira who was also in the elevator asked him with a mixture of astonishment and admiration from where he had learned to speak Chinese so well! To our point, this person found it more plausible that Mr. Carreira spoke fluent Chinese than that a person of Asian descent spoke Spanish.

In fact, Spanish speakers span the gamut of ethnic and racial backgrounds. Taking Cuba by way of example, Chinese laborers were brought to the island starting in the 1850s to work in the sugar fields. At its height, Havana's Barrio Chino (Chinatown) had a population of 40,000.[11] Cuba is also the home country of countless of descendants of African slaves, as well as descendants of immigrants from every corner of the world. From its music to its cuisine, religion, and art, Cuban culture is an amalgam of all these diverse influences. As Cuba goes, so does the rest of the Spanish-speaking world. Peru is home to descendants of European immigrants, African slaves, and Chinese laborers; Mexico, Chile, and Argentina have sizable populations of Germanic and Middle Eastern extraction, and so forth. Of course, Latin America is home to thousands of indigenous populations. Mexico alone has no fewer than 17 different indigenous groups with populations larger than 100,000.[12]

In the United States, immigrant children from Latin America with roots in other continents find it particularly difficult to define selves in reference to multiple ethnic groups. Two Asian Latinos, writer Fabiana Chiu-Rinaldi and student Du Kim Riu, describe some of such difficulties as follows:

Fabiana Chiu-Rinaldi: When I applied for a new Social Security card in Brooklyn, the form instructed me to check only one racial/ethnic category. I decided to be accurate and checked both Hispanic and Asian. Minutes after I turned in my form, the clerk, and later her supervisor, called me to their desks to try to persuade me to choose between the categories. After my tiresome recitation about who my parents were, what language we spoke, and what our last names were, they—fully confused—shrugged their shoulders and left the form unchanged. Unwilling to give in, I wanted every part of my identity, *China/Peruana*/Asian/Latina/American, to be counted and accounted for.[13]

Du Kim Riu: I was born and raised in a small country named Paraguay. I've lived in a multicultural world since the day I was born. I was Paraguayan during the day and Korean at night. When I came to America everything changed. I had to adapt to a new environment and culture. This is a very tough thing to do when you already have two cultures. Now I live as an American when I'm away from my family. When I'm home, back with my family, I'm Korean and Paraguayan. Learning a new culture and language wasn't as hard as I thought it would be, but keeping my identity has been hard. "José Pedro Kim Ryu" used to be my full name, but now I'm Du Kim Ryu. I don't own that Spanish name any more. Living in American is forcing me to lose my Paraguayan identity and replace it with an American one. When my parents are both Korean and when all my friends are all Americanized, it's hard to keep the Paraguayan identity that I had for 15 years. But I'm trying to preserve something of my original self—"*El Coreguayo*" as my old friends used to call me.

Labels—from the custom-made like "*Coreguayo*," to the ready-made like "Hispanic"—figure prominently in the lives of Latino youth as explained in the next section.

LABELS AND NAMES OF THE BORDERLANDS: A LEGEND

The Labels of the Borderlands

Latinos have different identification labels, some of their own creation or choice, and others imposed upon them on the basis of their looks, linguistic abilities, or preconceived notions. The term "Hispanic" was first used in the 1970s during the administration of President Richard Nixon in connection with the U.S. Census. Because this term has a negative connotation for some by virtue of its association with Spain and its colonial past in Latin America, the term "Latino" came into use in the 1990s. However, this term also has its share of critics; among them, journalist Rodolfo Acuña: "When and why the Latino identity came about is a more involved story. Essentially, politicians, the media, and marketers find it convenient to deal with the different U.S. Spanish-speaking people under one umbrella. However, many people with Spanish surnames contest the term *Latino*. They claim it is misleading because no Latino or Hispanic nationality exists since no Latino state exists, so generalizing the term *Latino* slights the various national identities included under the umbrella."[14]

Notwithstanding this criticism, Hispanic and Latino are increasingly used interchangeably and without political connotation. This is not the case with "Chicano," which, though strictly speaking refers to Americans of Mexican descent, has become politicized by its association with the Chicano Civil Rights Movement of the 1960s and 1970s. This movement inspired groundbreaking works of arts with a distinct social and political voice. One of its leading figures, Cherie Moraga, describes this voice as follows:

> I call myself a Chicana writer. Not a Mexican-American writer, not a Hispanic writer, not a half-breed writer. To be a Chicana is not merely to name one's racial/cultural identity, but also to name a politic, a politic that refuses assimilation into the U.S. mainstream. It acknowledges our mestizaje—Indian, Spanish, and *africano*.[15]

In keeping with this view, a Chicana student writes:

> One thing for sure is I have never been ashamed of being a *mexicana, chicana, latina,* or *hispana.* I have always been proud to be who I am in school and in society.

While terms like "Hispanic," "Latino," and even "Spanish-speaking" are meant to describe an ethnic group, in the United States, they are frequently used as a racial category. This is akin to using the term "American" as a proxy for race. Like the United States, Latin America is home to indigenous peoples, descendants of African slaves, and immigrants from all corners of the world. Some political figures of the 20th century attest to this diversity: the former Cuban president, Fulgencio Batista, was of Asian, black, and European descent; the former Peruvian president, Alberto Fujimori, was of Japanese descent, and the former Argentinean president, Carlos Menem, of Syrian descent. Bolivia's current president, Evo Morales, bears the distinction of being the first fully indigenous head of state in his country.

Notwithstanding the success of these and other individuals, the Spanish-speaking world has grappled with issues of racial prejudice, inequality, and discrimination throughout its history. Not surprisingly, these issues also afflict U.S. Latinos. In a national survey of Latinos, nearly half of respondents (47%) stated that Latino on Latino discrimination is a major problem. Another 36 percent stated it's a minor problem. The leading causes of discrimination cited in this survey include thus: different levels of income and education (41%), different countries (34%), and in a distant third, differences in skin color (8%).[16] It is important to remember, however, that issues surrounding discrimination generally do not fall into discrete categories. For example, the following comment speaks to the interrelatedness of issues of national origin, language, and customs and perspectives:

> For me, adapting to high school was very difficult. Not so much because of a language barrier as the diversity of Latinos and their customs that were very different than mine. I tried to adapt to them but I felt they were making fun of my point of view as a Colombian and that I didn't speak like them; I had a different accent.

Also interrelated are race and socioeconomic class. Though not generally viewed as white by mainstream Americans, significant numbers of U.S. Latinos describe themselves as such—as many as 53 percent, according to the 2010 U.S. Census. Many do so following a common practice in the Spanish-speaking world where being white is not solely associated with physical characteristics, but it is also linked to enjoying a higher socioeconomic status, level of education, professional success, and so on. Interestingly, this link leads to another use of the label "white" by U.S. Latinos, namely, as a pejorative term to put down Latinos who are perceived to be ashamed of their roots. Sociologist Jody Agius Vallejo, who has studied the latter use, offers insight into this phenomenon:

> On the one hand, middle-class Mexican Americans who grow up in low-income ethnic communities evince strong ethnic identities. These identities are reinforced by interactions with poorer relatives

and with non-Latinos who hold negative Latino stereotypes that are shaped by media and anti-immigrant politicians. On the other hand, those raised in middle-class households and white neighborhoods aren't tied as strongly to ethnic communities and they are more likely to view themselves, and are viewed by others, as "coconuts," "whitewashed," and "American," an identity that has historically been linked to whiteness.[17]

In the same vein, *Pocho* is a pejorative term used mainly by Mexicans in reference to Chicanos and other Latinos who are perceived as being too Americanized and who lack fluency in Spanish. Articulating a common view held by Mexicans abroad, writer and Nobel Prize winner Octavio Paz writes: "A Mexican sees a Chicano stuttering out his Spanish and thinks to himself—pocho—what an embarrassment."[18]

The sheer variety of labels used to strip Latinos of their ancestry or question their authenticity underscores the contentious nature of issues of identity among U.S. Latinos. The following comments speak to the struggles, as well as the coping strategies of Latino youth:

1. In high school I was one of very few Latinos. My friend and I were called the "Mexican kids." This was always funny to me because my Dad's family always told me I was American. In school I was labeled Mexican, but to the Mexicans, I am an American. I am part of each, but not fully accepted by either. In high school, I was considered Mexican because I spoke Spanish but I was considered "Pocho" by my Dad's family because my Spanish was not up to their standard. It's this weird duality in which you are stuck in the middle. Latinos are often told that they are not Americans but also that they are not connected to their heritage. You take pride in both cultures and learn to deal with the rejection. You may never be fully embraced by either side. That's why you seek out other people like yourself. Socializing with people who share a common experience helps you deal with this experience.

2. I would like to say I fall into the category of "perceived" Spanish speaker. My father had some extremely negative experiences growing up being Mexican so he made sure my first language was English hoping to save me similar troubles. But this created other negative experiences for me, mostly from Latinos. One girl in high school thought I was "white-washed" for not conversing in Spanish until I told her my family history. She had been avoiding me for three months and

acting very rude when I was around her. Her upbringing had led her to believe that any Latino who didn't speak Spanish didn't care about their culture.

The following comments illustrate the arbitrary and sometimes contradictory way in which identity labels are applied. The first student, a Spanish speaker, is labeled "white" by Latinos who do not speak the language. On the other hand, the second student is given that label, in part, on the basis of his inability to speak Spanish.

1. There are stereotypes about Hispanics that are very negative. There are times when people, trying to be nice tell me, "Oh, you're not Hispanic. You're more white than anything else." But I like my family background and heritage. Some of my friends who are Hispanic and don't know much Spanish wish that their parents taught them the language when they were young, like I was taught Spanish. If my parents hadn't spoken Spanish to me I wouldn't be the person I am today.

2. Throughout school I was usually the only student who was Hispanic that did not have a Spanish accent. I was also usually the only student to be born in the United States. This created some social problems around my friends. For instance, all of the Hispanic students thought I did not want to be Hispanic because I did not speak Spanish all that well. I also was looked down upon because I did not speak Spanish all that well. I also was looked down upon because when asked what nationality I was I would say, "I am Spanish." When I said this everyone thought that was the same as Mexican and I just did not want to say that I was Mexican because my grandmother was born in Madrid, not Mexico. If she was born in Mexico I would say I am Mexican. I do not have any shame in that, but students would make fun of me for that. They would say I want to be white and am ashamed of being Hispanic and Spanish is a better way of saying Mexican. All of this was very offensive to me.

While some U.S. Latinos use a national-origin label, such as Spanish, to define themselves, many prefer hyphenated labels, for the following reasons:

Don't call me Mexican. I have never lived there and I will never belong there. Call me a hyphenated American, a Mexican-American, a child of two worlds.

Overall, U.S. Latinos follow a progression of self-definitions from national origin to hyphenated American to American. Interestingly, Latino youth who experience discrimination on racial-ethnic grounds are less likely to identify as American and more likely to use national-origin identity labels. To sociologist Ruben Rumbaut, this indicates that discrimination and rejection undercut assimilation to the mainstream.[19]

NAMES IN THE BORDERLANDS

Like labels, proper names are closely aligned with issues of identity and evoke strong reactions among Latinos. Naming practices in the Spanish-speaking world differ considerably from those in the United States. In most Spanish-speaking countries, people have two last names. Taking the writer Gabriel García Márquez by way of example, his father's paternal last name is García and his mother's paternal last name is Márquez. Latin families also go by two last names, namely, the paternal last names of the father and mother. Hence, the family Gabriel García Márquez grew up in would be called the García Márquez family, whereas the family he created with his wife would have his first last name (García) and his wife's first last name. Dual names such as *José Luis* and *Ana Luisa* are also very common in the Spanish-speaking world.

Naming practices for married women in the Spanish-speaking world can vary slightly from one country to the next and by individual preference. Many women do not change their name when they marry. More traditional ones, however, may drop their maternal last name and adopt their husband's paternal last name. Following this practice, if María Pérez Ruiz marries José Arco Menéndez, she will be called María Pérez Ruiz de (of) Arco. However, this is a social practice rather than an official renaming. For official purposes, she retains her birth name.

In the United States, the practice of using dual first and last names presents some problems. In the Spanish-speaking world, last names are alphabetized by the paternal last name. Thus, in a Spanish bookstore, García Márquez's books would be found under "G." On the other hand, in the United States, where alphabetization is usually done by the second last name, his books would be shelved under "M." Seen as overly long, dual first and last names are often shortened in the United States for reasons of expediency. This seemingly innocuous practice can have unintended consequences. As a case in point, author Maria Carreira arrived in the United States with two first and last names. Maria Margarita Carreira Morán, the name she went by for the first 11 years of her life, was shortened to its current form by a teacher who jokingly explained that there were too many "r's." Eager to fit in, the child accepted this change without thinking through the consequences. What neither the teacher nor the child took into consideration at the time was that the dropped names were special to the author's mother—"Margarita" was the name of her mother (i.e., the author's grandmother) and Morán was her paternal last name. The loss of these two names—effectively, an erasure of her mother's presence—is now a source of regret for the author.

Children are often named after a parent, godparent, or a close relative to honor that person and establish a special connection. In the United States, this practice takes on the added meaning of serving as an overt marker of ethnic identity. The following student speaks to this issue:

> My name comes from my dad, who's also named José. My dad told me that he always dreamed of naming his first son José. I think this all has to do with a tradition among Latins whereby first-born children are named after their mom or dad. Having the name José makes me feel proud. It's a Biblical name, so I know where it comes from. I also like it because it's very common among Mexicans. In this way, my name identifies me as Mexican and that fills me up with pride. However, there is something that bothers me. It's not my name per se, but the way English speakers pronounce it. It's always bothered me that when my teachers do roll call, they say "Josei," instead of "José." I realize that it may be hard for them to pronounce my name right, by I'm José and not "Josei."

Religious names like Jesús, Angel, and Guadalupe, though commonplace in the Spanish-speaking world, can prove problematic in the United States as explained by the following students:[20]

1. Whenever I introduce myself, I brace for the giggles and smart-ass comments: Jesus . . . is that really your name? . . . Christ, is that your last name?

2. My complete name is María Guadalupe Pérez. As a young girl, I never felt embarrassed or nervous when my teachers would say my name on the first day of school. But over time I started to feel embarrassed of my name and I became "María." At home my name is Lupita but when my friend would call me by that name in school I used to get mad and feel uncomfortable. Sometimes I felt guilty for disliking my name, but I really wanted a "normal" name. After all these years and many classes

I thought by now I might feel more comfortable with my name. But nothing's changed. I feel trapped between what I am and what I wish I were. Every Dec. 12 I get calls from people wishing me a happy name-sake day (In the Catholic Church, Dec. 12 is the Virgin of Guadalupe Day). I like it that people are so sweet. But at the same time, I don't think I deserve it because I'm still embarrassed by my name. I think it's the pressure to be more American that makes me feel like this.

3. Angel, that's my name. It's a boy's name in Mexico and a girl's name in U.S. For me, it's just an embarrassing name. That's why I call myself Angelo sometimes, although it's not my real name.

Many Latinos blend Latin and American naming customs as a way of preserving their dual identity. Some hyphenate their two last names, and others use their maternal last name as a middle name. Often, first-generation parents choose bilingual names such as Daniel and Sandra, which can be said with a Spanish pronunciation at home and with an English pronunciation outside. Others take on English names for use outside the home, reserving their Spanish names for more intimate settings. For the following students, the practice of having a public and a private name goes hand in hand with having two identities:

1. As an American who's Latin, it has been difficult to choose the way in which I present my name. For example, at home I am known as Vero, not as Verónica. But when I am at school and work they call me Verónica. As the years have passed, I have become more used to the two different ways in which I present myself. The good thing about this is that I have the advantage of feeling like I am two different people; with Verónica I can be more professional and a bit more private whereas with Vero I feel more confident and happy and feel more at home. This is why it makes me feel beautiful to be part of the Latino culture because I have the advantage of having two completely different identities.

2. Everyone writes my name as if it were English (Rebecca) with two "c"s, but in reality, my name is Spanish and is written with only one "c" (Rebeca). When I was a kid, I used to change my name to the English spelling because I wanted to be like the others. My father, being American, would laugh and tell me that I was American and to spell it with two "c"s. But my mom said I was Mexican and I should spell it with one "c." Imagine how confusing it was for me hearing that. Yes, I

am American because I was born and raised here, but I am Latina and I spell my name with one "c."

While naming issues pose persistent challenges for Latinos, societal attitudes toward Spanish names appear to be changing for the better. Not too long ago, Latino public figures took on English names to be accepted by mainstream society. Thus, Ramón Gerardo Antonio Estévez changed his name to Martin Sheen when he started his career in the 1960s. A generation later, however, his son Emilio Estévez kept his Latino surname and also went on to find success. In politics, a Latino name can be a downright asset. California Representative Loretta Sánchez lost her bid for the Anaheim City Council as a Republican candidate using her Anglo married name, but then won a hotly contested Congressional district that was 65 percent Latino when she dropped her non-Latino married name and changed her political affiliation to Democrat.

Yet, as mainstream America has become more accepting of Spanish names, Latino parents are increasingly opting for English names for their children. Thus, in 2010, for the first time in more than two decades, "José" lost out to "Jacob" as the most popular boy's name in Texas. Other Spanish names like Ángel, Juan, Luis, Diego, and Jesús have also fallen in popularity, even as the Latino population continues to grow. Some experts believe that this is a measure of assimilation—or more precisely, as discussed next, *acculturation.*

THE CROSSROADS OF THE BORDERLANDS: ACCULTURATING TO AMERICAN SOCIETY

U.S. Latinos are acculturating to life in this country, that is, they are creating blended identities that enable them to effectively function in American society while maintaining their home culture. In this way, they are different from other immigrant groups, which have undergone assimilation, a process that involves giving up their home culture.

Acculturation serves Latino youth well by allowing them to draw on the best of both of their cultures. Cultural psychologists Marcelo and Carola Suárez Orozco present a model of culture that sheds light on this process. This model distinguishes between two domains of culture: the instrumental and the expressive. The instrumental domain encompasses skills, practices, and perspectives that are conducive to success in American society. The expressive domain encompasses elements that give people a sense of self, including cultural values, attitudes, and ways of relating to others.[21]

Crucially, both domains are significant to the well-being and success of Latino youth. In the realm of the instrumental, there's unanimous consent that immigrants must learn English and acquire skills that will give them access to good jobs and upward mobility. At the same time, in the realm of the expressive, Suárez Orozco and Suárez Orozco argue that immigrant children are generally best served by maintaining ties to their culture of origin. This is because immigrant cultures hold beliefs and attitudes that are conducive to success, such as respect of family and authority, deference for education, and optimism about the future. In addition, by holding on to their expressive culture, immigrant children can retain a sense of identity and social connectedness, both of which are crucial to their psychological well-being.

The following comment brings to light on another way in which acculturation contributes to the well-being of immigrant children, namely, by giving them the tools to manage the seemingly irreconcilable value systems and perspectives that coexist in the Borderlands.

Having been born in Los Angeles to Salvadorian parents, I can see both points of view—that of Americans as well as of immigrants. One thing I have noticed is that Latino parents usually don't have American friends and American parents, don't have Latino friends. Because these two groups don't get together, they don't get to know each other. My parents are very protective of me. When I lived at home, they always wanted to know where I was, who I was with, and what I was doing. Before allowing me to visit another friend's home, they would ask to speak to the parents and even then they would often insist that I return home before dark. The funny thing is that my parents didn't even realize that they were strict. They just thought that that was the normal way of being. This is because they only talked to other Latino parents who acted the same. They knew nothing about how American parents viewed things or behaved.

I had a friend Gabriela whose parents my friends had known for over ten years. One day, I asked them if I could sleep over at her house and they said "no." Another time, a friend named Karen asked to sleep over at our house. Karen just picked up her phone called her mom and told her mom that she wanted to spend the night at my house. Just like that, the mom said it was fine. My parents asked me when Karen's parents would be calling to talk to them. They became confused when I told them that they were not going to call. My father said: "And Karen's parents, don't they want to know about where their daughter is spending the night?" I told them that they already knew, because Karen had told them. Still confused, my dad insisted: "But don't they want to talk to us briefly to get to know us or to check that their daughter is not misleading them?" Karen asked me what was going on and I told her. I don't remember her exact words but she said something to the effect that my family was a little weird.

That's when I realized that my parents don't understand how they look to American parents. I realize that my parents did what they did to protect me. But Americans don't view this behavior as an act of caring. They view it as worrying about insignificant things.

The process of acculturation is especially daunting during the formative years, when children and youth struggle to find their place in the world. For many young Latinos, cultural ambivalence, identity disorientation, and anxiety over meeting competing expectations are part and parcel of the process.

1. As you stray away from the comfort zone of the family and into a world where you are looked at as not just different, but less than another "American child," you can visualize the struggles to be encountered for the rest of your life. You may say that not all White-Americans look down on Mexicans. While this is probably true, it feels otherwise. Since birth we begin a journey that's exciting because we can be part of two extraordinary cultures. Nonetheless, it is also difficult because White-Americans want us to assimilate into White culture but they can't comprehend that we can't do that because of our Mexican heritage. We are proud of who we are and where we came from.

2. As I progressed in my education I started speaking less Spanish and being less connected to my Mexican culture. I wasn't Mexican enough and was more "white washed!" I hated that! I wasn't much of anything really. I realized that being Mexican-American was hard. You have to be good at both cultures to be accepted in the world.

3. Who am I really? American or Hispanic? I have my own opinions about the two cultures. But sometimes I don't accept them. It's a total confusion in choosing my real identity and culture. I am always the same person, I am who I am, and sometimes I don't need either culture. It's more like I create my own culture, one which I will be able to give my future family.

4. Most children of Mexican parents live a double life. From the day they are born to the first day of school, they speak Spanish. Then, they enter school. At that point, it becomes about being American and speaking English most of the day and being Mexican and speaking Spanish at home. It's only when they get together with other children like them that they can be who they are.

5. Half of your day you spend in school, where all you do is write, read, and speak English. *Después llega la hora del almuerzo y estás allí con tus amigos* (then comes lunch and there you are with your friends) talking busting out your Spanglish. Once that bell rings you go back to English. Then it's time to go home and you have to change mindsets to *hablar y hablar en español con tus padres* (speak and speak Spanish to your parents). It's really hard to live that way. I can't imagine speaking English to my parents. They want me to maintain my *raíces* (roots), which come from my Mexican family.

6. Growing up Latina in the United States is a mixture of two cultures. I celebrate Halloween as well as *Día de los Muertos* and Three Kings Day. Despite all the stereotypes there are about Mexican-Americans, I am proud to be who I am . . . Latina.

7. I am an American raised with Hispanic values and beliefs. It has been a challenge trying to balance these two worlds. At home I would have to speak Spanish very well otherwise I would be a called a *pocho*. At school I had to speak proper English, if not, I would have been labeled as illiterate and not patriotic. Trying to balance these two distinctive cultures in my life was overwhelming.

8. I heard on the radio once a woman saying she and her family went to Tijuana and when they were crossing back into the United States immigration officials gave them a hard time. They would not let them cross the border because they had a Mexican flag on their car. The officials said they understood that they were proud of their nationality, but it was a lack of respect to enter the U.S. with that on their car and were told they would not be allowed to enter the country unless they removed it. After discussing it with the officials, they eventually gave in and took the flag down. Sometimes being of two nationalities can cause serious conflicts and controversies.

Though painful and difficult, the struggles relayed here are a normal part of the process of acculturation, which follows three stages: contact, conflict, and adaptation. In the contact stage, which happens when first exposed to the new culture, individuals can feel both overwhelmed and exhilarated by the differences. At the conflict stage, they wrestle with the differences, trying to strike a balance between them. At this point, feelings of betrayal to one's heritage can set in and last for a number of years. In the final stage of adaptation, decisions are made about what will be shed and what will be adopted. There are vast individual differences with regard to the pace of progression from one stage to the next, and not everyone reaches the third stage of acculturation. A range of factors are known to account for such differences, including age, personality, level of education, reasons for immigrating to the United States, the availability of support networks, and so on.[22]

Capturing snapshots of the process of acculturation, the following stories start out at the conflict stage and move toward adaptation.

1. When my friend was about to celebrate her 13th birthday, she and her mom began to plan a party. One day when my friend and her mom went out to buy things for the party, my friend said, "I want more American things!" Her mom began to think about what her daughter had said and decided to buy the things she wanted. She had many things to say to her daughter about her response, but she knew that her daughter would learn her lesson during her party. The party was small and limited to family and a few friends. Her family was Latino and they were hoping to have a normal birthday party like the ones they had—with tacos, toasted tortillas, salsa, and other Latino food. When her family saw the party food was hamburgers and hot dogs, they felt deceived. They asked my friend's mom why she choose this kind of food. My friend told them that there was a big part of her family and her culture that she didn't like. My friend saw that she had made her family sad, but more importantly she had betrayed her identity. After the party, my friend's mom said to her: "You can never change your culture or your family. We are who we are." Now-a-days my friend is proud of her family and her culture.

2. I used to be embarrassed of being Mexican. I used to dress like my Anglo friends and listen to their music. The only way I could be like them was by hiding my identity and changing who I was. I think society wants children of all nationalities to be just like Anglo children. That's how I lost my culture. But it's no longer like that. Now I am proud to be Mexican and I love to speak Spanish. I'm glad I didn't forget my Spanish. I want to continue to learn more about my home language and culture.

3. The longer I lived there (Ohio), the more I strived to shed all of my Cuban-ness. I wanted to be white, skinny, and not curvy and I did not want to have an accent. So I did everything I could to get rid of it all. Gone were the accent and the salsa music. In came the American Eagle clothes, American accent, and bubbly pop music. I lost who I really was. Once I left that place and moved to California and I finally grew some confidence. I realized one thing, I was sad. I was sad that I had let these people take my heritage and my culture away from me. Sad that I had let them take away a huge chunk of who I was.

Gender roles and issues of sexuality pose significant challenges to the process of acculturation. Young women, in particular, walk a tight rope between the expectations of the home and those of American society. In many situations, including the following one, loving parents and children are unable to find common ground despite their best efforts.

Latino parents often want to impose on their children the values and practices that their parents imposed on them. They are particularly strict with their daughters. I love my parents, but I wish they would be a little more approving of my decisions. I try to explain to my mom that things are different here, but she doesn't understand. I remember when I decided to risk it and tell my mom that I wanted to move in with my boyfriend of five years. I didn't know exactly how she was going to react, but I had a hunch that it wouldn't be well. Sure enough, she waited for a minute or two and then said: Oh no, not before marriage.

Deep inside I feared that my mom would never think of me the same way. We feel very differently about so many things, and this is one of them. After seeing the fear and sadness on her face, I nervously tried to explain to her why I wanted to live with my boyfriend. I told her that I wanted to live with him because I wanted to know what it was like to be around him all the time. I explain that I didn't want to rush into marriage and being so young, that I didn't feel that it was a good idea for us to get married yet. With every sentence I said, she became more confused and sad. I told her that I didn't understand why this hurt her so much. I explained that things are different in this country and in my generation. I said that I knew people that had lived together before getting married who went on to have a wonderful marriage. I told her that I loved him and trusted him very much. I added that he and I were very responsible and mature, that we had known each other for a long time, that we were serious about marriage in the future and wanted to prepare for it.

But my mom didn't budge. She said: it would make me much happier if you married him before living with him. She reasoned that since we had already been together for so long we should go ahead and get married. She said that my father would have a hard time accepting this and added that she had heard of couples who had broken up after moving in together. I told her that this wouldn't happen to us and I explained that I wanted to get my degree before getting married.

Eventually, I had no choice but to point out that as an adult I was entitled to make my own decisions. I love and respect my parents but I believe that living with him before marriage is in my best interest. Sometimes Latin parents don't allow their children to grow. They restrict their freedom only because of old customs and beliefs that they learned as children.

DANGER ZONES: DISCRIMINATION AND STEREOTYPING

Acculturation—a desirable outcome for Latino youth for the reasons put forth earlier—can be undercut by experiences of discrimination. Such experiences are the focus of this section. A Latina grandmother interviewed for this book describes one particularly painful experience of this type from her youth:

> When we were in Texas, there were signs in the restaurant that read "No Dogs or Mexicans." I am of Irish descent and my husband is a Spaniard (Basque) and was brought here when he was young to work on the cattle farms in Texas. In 1963 or 1964, we were travelling through Texas and we sat down to eat at a restaurant. We were tired from travelling and we had our 2-year-old son with us, who was hungry. We waited and waited, but we were not served. When we finally complained, we were told that they did not serve Mexicans.

Though incidents such as these may be rare nowadays, issues of race and ethnic stereotyping loom large for many Latinos. Research shows that Latino children are keenly aware of prejudice and negative stereotyping. For example, asked to complete the sentence: Most Americans think that [people from my country] are _____, Latino children in one study gave the following answers[23]:

Most Americans think that we can't do the same things as them in school or at work. (10-year-old Mexican girl)

Most Americans think that we are lazy, gangsters, drug-addicts that only come to take their jobs away. (14-year-old Mexican boy)

Most Americans think that we don't exist. (12-year-old Mexican boy)

Most Americans think we're useless. (14-year-old Dominican girl)

Most Americans think that we are garbage. (14-year-old Dominican boy)

Most Americans think that we are members of gangs. (9-year-old Central American girl)

Even passing encounters with discrimination can have a profound effect on children. Witnessing discrimination against one's group, without being personally victimized by it, can lead to depressed emotion and lower self-esteem.[24] It's also conceivable that such experiences can lead to feelings of guilt, similar to those experienced by survivors of traumatic events. Putting oneself in the place of this student, it is easy to understand why this is the case.

Whenever my Mexican looking friends and I would go somewhere people would often give us looks or we would constantly get hassled by the police. Sometimes white people would see our group they would directly come to me to ask a question instead of my Hispanic looking friend. I was working for a detail business once and while my boss (Mexican American) and I were washing cars, although it was his business and he looked older people kept coming up to me for questions or directions. People would simply come to me for answers because I looked white.

As noted earlier, Latinos' own in-group stereotypes and discriminatory practices pose significant problems as well. The following comment speaks to the devastating double-sided rejection often experienced by non-stereotypical Latino children:

Specific events that led to an increased awareness of different races were introduced early in my childhood. I lived in an Anglo-dominated neighborhood and when playing soccer on the streets in my neighborhood I noticed other kids playing basketball. When I asked if I could join them I was mostly ignored. I would have to walk eight blocks towards the ghetto to have no problem socializing with others and play a fun game of soccer. Even then I would run into problems because I wasn't "authentically" from the neighborhood and was looked at as inferior. I was lost in my ethnic identity because I wasn't Mexican to be accepted by fellow Latinos and I was too brown to play with the children in my neighborhood.

Recalling the experiences of the Asian Latinos cited at the beginning of this chapter, the following students struggle with stereotypes about what real Latinos look like. For some, such stereotypes render them invisible to other Latinos.

1. Growing up no one could physically tell I was Peruvian. I have blonde hair and green eyes. Most people stereotype what Hispanics look like. I remember growing up embarrassed that my family was not American. I remember in high school a boy that I liked called my house and my grandma picked up the phone and started speaking to him in Spanish. I was embarrassed because he had no idea what she was saying.

2. People don't believe I speak Spanish. My parents are from Mexico and Guatemala but because of the way my eyes are shaped, I look Filipino.

3. It feels good to speak Spanish. As a Latina it is easier because it is encouraged, which I like. But I'm not your typical Latina either. Since I'm half African-American, people usually think I'm Puerto Rican or Panamanian, but I'm Mexican and people don't even see it coming, not even Mexican people.

4. People often tell me that I have features of a black person like the big nose and the big lips. But one thing they never figure out is that I am actually Mexican. People are shocked when I speak Spanish.

ROUTES AND PATHWAYS TO WELL-BEING

It's well known that having a strong sense of ethnic identity helps some Latino children cope with discrimination and stereotyping. Experts Adriana J. Umaña-Taylor, Marcelo Diversi, and Mark A. Fine explain why:

One possibility is that individuals who have a strong ethnic identity are aware of discrimination and oppression toward their group, and when they are confronted with negative remarks, they attribute those remarks to prejudiced attitudes of others as opposed to some internal characteristic of themselves. Thus, this does not negatively affect their self-esteem. On the other hand, individuals with a weak ethnic identity (e.g., unexplored and uncommitted), when faced with a negative remark may take it personally and believe that it is some internal quality of theirs that justifies the negative remarks. Their self-esteem may be negatively affected by what could be thought of as ignorance or prejudice toward their own ethnic group.[25]

The empowering effects of ethnic identity for Latino youth are on display in the following comments:

1. In order to succeed in life you have to take pride in your roots. You can't move forward if you are ashamed of where you come from. Latino youth need to know their culture and that of Latinos from other countries or regions in the US.

2. Being Mexican and coming from a family of eleven (including my parents), we have every color of skin at home. The funny thing is that the seven brothers and sisters that were born in Mexico are light skinned and what some might consider "American looking." The three that were born here (including myself) are *morenos* (dark). Now, I'm very proud of my skin color, but it is the stereotypical color that everyone associates with Mexicans and other Latinos. But the great thing about being Mexican is that we come in all colors. In my family we joke about it the fact that we don't look like we're related. People will say: "really, that is your sister? . . . *nada que ver*" (not even close). My father is light-skinned and green-eyed and my mother is *morena*. Together, they have created very beautiful *hijos*.

3. Growing up in Ecuador, I never felt like an outsider. Latinos love to show off their culture. Thus, when it came for the class of 2005 to paint on the pavement of the school (since it was a tradition of every class), most of the Latinos wanted to put a flag next to their names to show pride for their culture. Yet when it was all done and ready, the school authority removed such object because simply we were not allowed to identify ourselves that way. Now I did not attend the painting, but it didn't stop me from showing resentment for the act. To me, it was like who was anybody to tell me what and who I can identify with, especially with something like mi cultura that I lived and

breathed back in Ecuador. My identity is formed not only by my person, but my mentality, my past, and my future. Hindering students or anyone to certain restrictions of how they can identify with just adds on to the "awkwardness" among Latinos and those of other races. After all, how can one live in tranquility when it comes to one's heritage one cannot express themselves in such a way that demonstrates pride?

Besides ethnic pride, these comments illustrate another tool of empowerment used by Latino youth—resilience. Resilience is the capacity to tap into personal, cultural, and social resources for maintaining well-being and finding meaning under difficult situations. Personal strengths associated with resilience are as follows: (1) problem solving, which includes planning, flexibility, resourcefulness, critical consciousness and insights; (2) social competence, which includes responsiveness, cross-cultural communication skills, empathy and caring, forgiveness, altruism; (3) autonomy, which includes positive identity, self-efficacy and mastery, adaptive distancing and resistance, self-awareness and mindfulness, humor; and (4) sense of purpose, which includes goal direction, special interest, optimism, hope, sense of meaning.[26]

All of these traits can be learned and developed by anyone, under the right circumstances. Supportive and nurturing relationships, confidence-building experiences, and access to positive role models are critical in this regard.[27] Many methods for teaching resilience use skits, role-play, and short stories, to raise awareness of and practice strategies.

The following comments illustrate a variety of strategies of resilience and in a classroom can serve to prompt a discussion on resilience. Unlike the earlier cited examples from a study where students completed the prompt "most Americans think that," these comments don't stop with a mere listing of negatives. They also offer solutions, which is at the core of resilience.

AUTONOMY, OPTIMISM, AND SENSE OF PURPOSE

The advice I would give to Latino students is that they should work as hard as they can to reach their goals and they should stand up for themselves and not let people push them around. They should not pay attention to people that say that they cannot do something just because they're Mexican or Latino. Just stay positive and set your focus on showing the world what you are capable of.

CRITICAL CONSCIOUSNESS, ADAPTIVE
DISTANCING, AND RESISTANCE

1. Many times Latinos are unappreciated because of the way we speak English, because we have an accent when we speak, or because we don't speak English at all. I believe we are looked at as ignorant and silly people because we don't know how to express ourselves well in English. But the same people who criticize us don't speak English correctly the way they expect us to.

2. Latinos in this country are treated, seen, and criticized differently just because we have brown skin and dark hair. They treat us as if we are not as good as them. Just because Americans speak the most important language in the world doesn't give them the right to talk down to Latinos.

3. Many Latinos immigrate to this country to improve their lives. Unfortunately, we come across things that take us down a bad path that don't allow us to focus on our goals such as prejudice for not learning the new language fast enough and attacking us for having a different culture.

Seen from the perspective of resilience theory, seemingly ordinary actions and choices taken by Latino youth emerge as truly remarkable. For example, in the anecdotes that follow, the decision to remain silent in the face of an insulting comment is not driven by weakness or passivity, but by a strategic objective to make the best of a very difficult situation.

1. A few years ago my family took a road trip through Utah over the Christmas holidays. At first, Utah seemed like a paradise, full of natural beauty and free of the problems of city life. It seemed that this would be the perfect vacation spot for our family. But things did not turn out so well. An incident at a store will forever remain in my memory. My cousin and my little sister and I went to the corner store to buy some treats. While standing in line to pay, a man behind us sneezed and I said to him "Bless you." Much to my surprise, he gave the children and me a look of disgust. Not liking this, we decided to leave the store. As we reached the door, we heard the man say that Mexicans were dirty and that we should all go back to Mexico. I resolved that I would be respectful to a fault and told him he should think about how his words would impact the children. When we got home I explained to the children that this man was ignorant and said

these things because he didn't know Mexicans. I explained that even when people are disrespectful to us, we should be respectful to them. Most of all, I made sure that the children understood that Mexicans are not dirty, but that we are respectful people. That day, I learned how to deal with Americans who say insulting things in front of Mexicans who understand English.

2. I work in a very busy emergency room and sometimes I need to translate for patients. One patient I was working with was able to understand some of the questions the doctor posed to her in English. When he realized this he asked the patient if she understood him. Shyly, she said, "Yes, a little bit." The doctor then replied in a rude and angry tone, "Then you don't need to speak Spanish, do you?" Unfortunately, they are the ones that sign my paycheck and because this job is such a great experience, I can't make any complaints about the doctors until I get into med school. I suffer silently, watching as my community is mistreated and degraded on a daily basis.

Closely related to the concept of resilience is agency or the ability of individuals to act independently and to make their own free choices rather than accept the limitations of structural factors such as social class, gender, ethnicity, language, and so on. Agency enables individuals to tap into personal and community resources to overcome adversity and achieve well-being.[28]

Together, agency and resilience enable this young Latino to rise above crushing circumstances and succeed against the odds.

My parents took me to the local school, but due to the overcrowding of classes I had to take the bus to an elementary school in San Pedro, CA. This school was composed of predominantly white students, and I ended up in this school because this was the only school that was accepting students from overcrowded schools. The LAUSD system at that time was so unorganized that a friend and I were the only Spanish-speaking students in the classroom. All I can remember from the three months at this elementary school was that my classmates would call me names such as *wetback, beaner,* and Mexican.

Racial comments against me did not cease after I was transferred to a local elementary school. Racism from my own people emerged and continued through high school. The poor education system also influenced on how the ESL children were seen, we didn't have rights for a better education. ESL children were put in these classes for the simple fact that the primary language spoken at home was Spanish. The problem here was that the program was not suited or the personnel were not trained correctly to teach English to the Spanish-speaking immigrants. Although the ESL program placed a burden on my education, I've been able to return to school and currently I'm on my last semester at the university. Racist comments or looks have continued but with the help of my knowledge I've managed how to control my emotions and judge racist people as ignorant.

THE MAIN ATTRACTIONS: CUSTOMS AND TRADITIONS

The Borderlands are rich in celebrations and traditions. Here, time-honored festivities from every corner of the Spanish-speaking world and newly minted ones mark the seasons and honor the Latino presence in the United States.

Many Latino traditions and celebrations are rooted in religion. This is because Latinos, as a group, are religious and see religion and cultural values as inextricably linked.[29] Research indicates that religion is a positive force in the life of Latino youth. Not only do those who attend church or consider their faith to be important have higher grades than those who don't, they also enjoy better relationships with their teachers and peers.[30] The following anecdote underscores the importance of understanding and respecting Latino religious practices:

A few years ago when I was in the twelfth grade in high school, I remember asking my English teacher, who was an Anglo-Saxon lady, if I could take the exam that we were going to have the next day, until the day after because I knew that I was going to be absent the day of the exam since it was going to be Ash Wednesday and my grandma makes us all go to church in the morning and get some ash that the priest puts in our foreheads. So I explained that to Mrs. Smith and I asked her if she would let me take the exam on Thursday but she refused my petition by telling me "No, if you want to take the exam you need to be here the day of the exam, besides ash on your forehead is not going to get you into a good university, but a well-written essay for sure will, tell that to your grandma." After knowing that Ms. Smith wouldn't give me a make-up exam I explained everything to my grandma and I told her that I wasn't going to miss class for going to church but she scolded me and said that I was going to go to church because that was my responsibility and duty as a

Catholic. So at the end I went to church and I got a zero in my exam. Luckily I was still able to get an "A" in my class but I had to do many extra credit projects and study really hard for the next exams in order to get the highest grades possible. So I have experienced that disparity between both cultures, a difference that many teachers are not aware of or like Mrs. Smith, do not understand or value.

The Christmas holidays are a particularly important time in the Spanish-speaking countries. Much more so than in the United States, these holidays are about spending time with friends and family and honoring their religious significance. One of the most popular celebrations leading up to Christmas, *Las Posadas,* reenacts the biblical story of Mary and Joseph's search for lodging as they traveled to Bethlehem, where Jesus was born. For the nine nights leading up to Christmas, adults and children dressed as shepherds, angels, and Mary and Joseph gather before a neighborhood home asking for shelter and singing Christmas carols. The hosts reply with a song, opening their home to their guests, serving them treats, and offering lodging. The last *posada,* held on December 24, is followed by midnight mass. In keeping with American practice, many U.S. Latino children receive their presents on Christmas day. Traditionally, however, children in the Spanish-speaking world receive their presents on January 6, the *Día de los Reyes Magos* (Three Kings Day), the Feast of the Epiphany, when the Three Wise Men presented their gifts to the baby Jesus.

For many youth, these and other traditions are more than just celebrations harking back to another time and place. As explained here, these practices are at the core of *Latinidad,* or what it means to be a Latino:

1. I love to celebrate Christmas Mexican style. This is something beautiful that I treasure much about my culture. The best thing about it is that that family and friends get together to celebrate. The festivities start a month in advance, first with the posadas. We set up the nativity scene and then the Christmas tree. Mexican style Christmas is celebrated with *tamales, buñuelos,* and *Champurrado.* Aunts, uncles, cousins, grandparents all get together on the 24th of December, which is called *"Noche Buena."* The celebration starts out with a prayer, we pray to the newborn Christ and we render Him honor. After that, we have a great feast. After we're done eating, the party is not over—we dance until exactly a minute before midnight. When the clock strikes 12:00, we hug each other and bring out a piñata and sweets. We open our presents and the party continues until 1:00 or 2:00 am. Every year

we do the same. This is my favorite of all our traditions. I wouldn't feel it was Christmas if I didn't celebrate it this way.

2. One time I dated an American with green eyes and dark hair and I always felt there was a cultural barrier between us. At first, I didn't want him to recognize that I was Mexican; I always claimed that I was a Spaniard. It was as if he had his own notions about Mexicans. Additionally, he wasn't able to share in my cultural experiences, such as the importance of a *Quinceañera* for Hispanic women. He didn't understand *Día de los Muertos* nor Three Kings Day. I explained to him that I couldn't stop feeling that these events meant nothing to him.

On *Día de los Muertos* (The Day of the Dead), Mexicans honor their deceased loved ones. Originating some 3,000 years ago as an Aztec celebration that mocked death, *Día de los Muertos* was originally held in the ninth month of the Aztec Solar Calendar (August, for us). However, with the conversion of the indigenous people to Catholicism, *Día de los Muertos* merged with All Souls' Day and came to be celebrated on November 2, blending Catholic and indigenous beliefs.[31] Undergoing a new change, in the United States, the *Día de los Muertos* is increasingly associated with the celebration of Halloween.

The *Quinceañera,* celebrated on a girl's 15th birthday, is the Latin version of the Sweet Sixteen party or a Debutant ball. Typically, the festivities require service to the community and include a religious ceremony in which a girl reaffirms her commitment to her faith, followed by a party that resembles a wedding reception with dinner, dancing, and attendants. Often, the girl and her attendants wear long gowns and are escorted by young men in tuxedos. Many families save money for years for this event, which can be as costly as a wedding. While originally a Mexican tradition, the *Quinceañera* is celebrated in other Latin American countries and is particularly popular among Latino families in the United States.

The United States has also given birth to new Latino traditions. What is today Latino Heritage Month (also known as National Hispanic Heritage Month) started out as a weeklong celebration under President Lyndon B. Johnson in 1968 to honor the contributions of American citizens "whose ancestors came from Spain, Mexico, the Caribbean and Central and South America."[32] It became a month-long celebration in 1988 under President Ronald Reagan. September 15 was chosen as the start of this celebration because it is the date when five Latin American countries gained their independence from Spain (Costa Rica, El Salvador, Guatemala, Honduras, and Nicaragua).

Cinco de Mayo (the Fifth of May) commemorates the Battle of Puebla in 1862 where the Mexican Army defeated the French in what was a key turning point toward Mexico's independence. A regional holiday in Mexico, *Cinco de Mayo* has taken on a larger significance in the United States, where it is a celebration of Mexican heritage, much in the same way that St. Patrick's Day is a celebration of Irish Americans.[33]

Other celebrations of national pride include the annual Puerto Rican Day Parade and Dominican Day Parade, both in New York City, the Cuban-American Heritage Festival in Key West Florida, and the National Celebration, observed by Salvadorian Americans throughout the country.

Behind these celebrations are countless Latino social and civic clubs committed to preserving cultural traditions and passing them on to future generations. Such organizations also sponsor a wide range of activities that are part of the social life of Latino communities in the United States, such as pageants, sports events, and local festivals. Among these, school clubs that cater to Latinos are particularly important by virtue of their ability to instill ethnic pride and provide the kind of social support that promotes engagement in children. The following comment elucidates some of the benefits of these associations.

At my school I was in the Spanish club. In this club we would organize fundraisers, such as selling Mexican food once a week, putting together a *folklórico Cinco de Mayo* celebration. By being involved in this club I stay true to my heritage and practice my Spanish with the other members of the group. I never came across other Spanish speakers unless it was other Spanish-club members. To me, not wanting to speak Spanish, which is my family's language, is like rejecting my family's culture and not accepting their traditions in my life. It is an honor to be part of this Mexican culture which I'm going to keep in my future family as well. I'm going to observe the traditions, discipline, morality, and language that my family taught me and make it part of my kids' life.

For college students, major specific organizations such as the Hispanic Business Students Association provide much-needed academic and social support in culturally appropriate and meaningful ways. Similar organizations exist for working professionals, such as the Hispanic Business Association and the Society of Hispanic Professional Engineers. There are also legal and charitable organizations that specialize in helping Latinos. Major ones are listed in the Resources section at the end of this chapter.

EVER-EXPANDING BORDERS

Like any overview of Latino culture in the United States, this one cannot hope to capture the full range of perspectives and experiences that characterize the Borderlands. We close this chapter with a commentary that underscores the complex and elusive nature of U.S. Latino identity and foreshadows the future of America.

A landmark of today's Borderlands, the labels examined in this chapter may soon be a thing of the past. A study by the Pew Research Center explains why:

> By 2050, will our racial categories still make much sense? These days our old labels are having trouble keeping up with our new weddings. A half century ago racial intermarriage was illegal in a third of the states and a gasp-inducing taboo just about everywhere else. Today, nearly one-in-six newlyweds marry across racial or ethnic lines.[34]

The following essay offers a miniature picture of what the Pew Research Center tells us will become an increasingly common American landscape. Written by Alicia Menéndez, a child of intermarriage and a host and producer at the *Huffington Post*, this piece is featured on the Pew Research Center website as a companion to a national survey of Latino identity.[35]

> It's easiest to imagine my non-Hispanic white mother's role in my Latina identity as the "absence of." If I'd had a Latina mother, the logic goes, I would speak fluent Spanish. I would have a proper reverse hyphenated surname, not the middle name "Jacobsen" that falls like an awkward feminist disclaimer between the very Latin "Alicia" and "Menéndez." But in reality, much of my Hispanic identity is the product of my Irish-German-Norwegian, third generation New Jersey mother, Jane, who swears that she was Dominican in her previous life.
>
> Jane's first contribution to my identity was her proactive choice to raise us in the same place she and my father grew up. Take exit 17 off the Turnpike, the last exit before the Lincoln Tunnel, make a right by the Toys "R" Us onto Kennedy Boulevard and you'll find yourself in the most densely populated city in America, Union City, New Jersey. The first wave of Hispanics who came to the "embroidery

capital of the world" were Cuban exiles, among them, my paternal grandparents, aunt and uncle. By the time my brother and I were in middle school, many of the Cubans had moved up and out, and were replaced with new waves of Dominicans, Puerto Ricans, Colombians and Ecuadorians.

If you grow up in Union City, you are likely, by default, to be effectively Hispanic. You learn to salsa by middle school. On at least one birthday, you'll be honored with an actual "Barby" (the kind they sell at the 99 cents store, not to be confused with Mattel's "Barbie") popping out of your cake. And you'll find it odd later in life when people say hello without cheek-to-cheek kisses.

If I'd had another mother, even a Latina mother, who wanted to uproot us from Union City, all of that cultural nuance would have been lost. At home, my mother's efforts were never forceful or overt. She simply loved Hispanic culture and she expressed that with authenticity and genuine curiosity. My mom is the one who put Isabel Allende books in my hands. She is the one who knew, long before he won a Pulitzer, that Junot Díaz was going to be a big deal. She's the one who makes café con leche every morning.

Yes, I bury my head in my hands every time my mother proudly declares that the only Spanish she knows is "Una cerveza, por favor." I laugh every time an email from "Juana" pops up in my inbox, or my mom calls me from her car phone to say that she's "bachat'ing up the Turnpike." But the truth is that without my gringa mother, I might not be as proud to be Latina as I am today.

DISCUSSION QUESTIONS

1. The following student describes the fusion of Mexican and American cultures as a cruel reality that leads to loss. Do you agree? In your opinion, is the kind of situation being described one consistent with assimilation or acculturation?

It's not just Spanish that starts to change, but also the customs and traditions. *Cinco de Mayo* is a celebration of Mexican identity, but ask the people celebrating this day about what actually happened on the 5th of May or when Mexican Independence Day is and they'll give you a blank look. Mexican food is also forgotten as it fuses with American cuisine. *Tacos, burritos, nachos and empanadas,* which derive from real Mexican dishes, have morphed in the US into something unrecognizable. In less than one generation, Mexican-American children lose their taste for *menudo* and *champurrado* and turn to pizzas and hamburgers. Like a soup, the mixture of so many cultures in Los Angeles leads to the loss of flavor of the original ingredients. This is the cruel reality faced many Latinos.

2. Sociologist Ruben Rumbaut writes:

Ethnic self-identities can be understood as "definitions of the situation of the self." For children of immigrants, they emerge from the interplay of racial and ethnic labels and categories imposed by the external society and the original identifications and ancestral attachments asserted by the newcomers. They are contextually malleable and may be hypothesized to vary across different social situations, across different developmental stages throughout the life course, and across different historical contexts.[36]

Which of the properties of ethnic self-identity are on display in the comments in this chapter? Which ones are not? Can you think of experiences from your own life that exemplify the missing ones?

3. Consider the following comment by Latino writer Richard Rodríguez.
What is the point being made about skin color? Do you agree? Are there other personal attributes that acquire significance from the context of life? Thinking back to Chapter 2, is bilingualism one such attribute?

The registration clerk in London wonders if I have just been to Switzerland. And the man who carries my luggage in New York guesses the Caribbean. My complexion becomes a mark of my leisure. Yet no one would regard my complexion the same way if I entered such hotels through the service entrance. That is only to say that my complexion assumes its significance from the context of my life.[37]

RESOURCES

Hispanic Association of Colleges and Universities (http://www.hacu.org)
A professional organization that aims to provide access to quality education to Hispanics and to "meet the needs of business, industry, and government through the development and sharing of resources, information and expertise."

Latin America's Professional Network (http://www.latpro.com)
A job search board to connect Hispanics and bilinguals with jobs and companies that support and promote diversity.

League of Latin American Citizens (LULAC) (http://www.lulac.org)
A Hispanic organization that advances the economic condition, educational
attainment, political influence, health, and civil rights of Hispanic Americans through community-based programs.

Mexican-American Legal Defense and Educational Fund (MALDEF) (http://
www.maldef.org)
A civil rights organization dedicated to bringing Latinos "into the mainstream of
American political and socio-economic life; providing better educational
opportunities; encouraging participation in all aspects of society."

The National Council of La Raza (http://www.nclr.org)
A civil rights advocacy, they provide assistance to Latinos in 41 U.S. states,
Puerto Rico, and Washington, D.C., in five areas—assets and investments,
civil rights and immigration, education, employment and economic status,
and health.

NOTES

1. Ana Castillo, *The Massacre of the Dreamers: Essays on Xicanisma*. New York: Plume, 1994.
2. Carlos Fuentes, *Valiente Mundo Nuevo*. Mexico, DF: Lectorum, 1990.
3. Gloria Anzaldúa, *Borderlands: La Frontera. The New Mestiza*. San Francisco: Aunt Lute Books, 1999.
4. Paul Taylor, Mark Hugo Lopez, Jessica Martinez, and Gabriel Velasco, "When Labels Don't Fit: Hispanics and Their Views of Identity." *Pew Hispanic Center,* April 4, 2012. http://www.pewhispanic.org/2012/04/04/when-labels-dont-fit-hispanics-and-their-views-of-identity/.
5. "Changing Faiths: Latinos and the Transformation of American Religion." *Pew Hispanic Center,* April 25, 2007. http://www.pewhispanic.org/2007/04/25/changing-faiths-latinos-and-the-transformation-of-american-religion.
6. "Hispanic Americans by the Numbers." *U.S. Census Bureau,* 2007. http://www.infoplease.com/spot/hhmcensus1.html.
7. The Bracero program was a guestworker program started in World War II to import Mexican immigrants to work as U.S. farmworkers.
8. The Marielitos were immigrants who fled during Cuba's economic downturn in the 1980s. Disproportionate numbers of Marielitos were released from Cuban jails and mental health facilities. The Balseros fled Cuba in rafts when the former Soviet Union withdrew economic support, plunging the island into deeper economic problems. The group gets its name from the Spanish word for raft "balsa."
9. U.S. Census Bureau, 2007. http://www.infoplease.com/spot/hhmcensus1.html.
10. Ibid.
11. "Barrio Chino: Chinatown in the Caribbean." *Chinese Historical and Cultural Project,* n.d. http://chcp.org/virtual-museum-library/barrio-chino-chinatown-in-the-caribbean/

12. "Derecho a Igulidad de Género: Resultado de Las Convocatorias 2014." Accessed April 29, 2014. http://www.cdi.gob.mx/index.php?id_seccion=660.

13. Fabiana Chiu-Rinaldi, "China Latina." In *Re-Collecting Early Asian America: Essays in Cultural Histo,* edited by Josephine Lee, Imogene L. Lim, and Yuko Matsukawa, 183. Philadelphia: Temple University Press, 2002.

14. Rodolfo Acuña, *U.S. Latino issues.* Westport, CT: Greenwood Publishing Group, 2003.

15. Cherie Moraga, "Art in America Con Acento." In *Latina. Women's Voices from the Borderlands,* edited by Castillo-Speed, Lillian, 211–20. New York: Simon & Schuster. A Touchstone Book, 1995.

16. Richard Fry, "Latinos in Higher Education: Many Enroll, Too Few Graduate." *Pew Hispanic Center,* September 5, 2002. http://www.pewhispanic.org/2002/09/05/latinos-in-higher-education.

17. Jody Agius Vallejo, "Latino Ethnicity and America's Future." *Pew Hispanic Center,* June 8, 2012. http://www.pewhispanic.org/2012/06/08/jody-agius-vallejo-latino-ethnicity-and-americas-future.

18. Octavio Paz, *El Laberinto de La Soledad: Fondo de Cultura Económica y Otras Obras.* New York: Penguin Books, 1997.

19. Thomas S. Weiner, ed., *Discovering Successful Pathways in Children's Development: Mixed Methods in the Study of Childhood and Family Life.* Chicago: University of Chicago Press, 2005.

20. "María" can function as a middle name for men, as for example, in the case of former Spanish prime minister, José María Aznar. Likewise, José can be a female middle name, as is the case with tennis pro María José Matínez Sánchez.

21. Marcelo Suárez Orozco and Carola Suárez Orozco, *Children of Immigration.* Cambridge, MA: Harvard University Press, 2001.

22. Jean Phinney, "Ethnic Identity and Acculturation." In *Acculturation: Advances in Theory, Measurement, and Applied Research,* edited by K. Chun, P. Organista, and G. Marin, 63–81. Washington, DC: American Psychological Association, 2003.

23. Suárez Orozco and Suárez Orozco, *Children of Immigration.*

24. Shannon K. Mc McCoy and Brenda Major, "Group Identification Moderates Emotional Responses to Perceived Prejudice." *Personality and Social Psychology Bulletin* 29 (2003): 1005–17.

25. Adriana J. Umaña-Taylor, Marcelo Diversi, and Mark A. Fine, "Ethnic Identity and Self-Esteem of Latino Adolescents: Distinctions among the Latino Populations." *Journal of Adolescent Research* 17 (2002):303.

26. Michael Ungar, "Resilience across Cultures." *British Journal of Social Work* 38 (2008):218–35.

27. Ibid.

28. Ibid.

29. The Center for Migration Studies. *Welcome! Pastoral Response to Hispanic Immigrants.* Staten Island, NY: Coast Specialty Printing Company, 2007.

30. David Sikkink and Edwin I. Hernández, "Religion Matters: Predicting School Success among Latino Youth." *Interim Reports* 1 (January 2003).

31. Carlos Miller, "Day of the Dead History: Indigenous People Wouldn't Let 'Day of the Dead' Die." *The Arizona Republic,* September 5, 2008, sec. Entertainment. http://www.azcentral.com/ent/dead/articles/dead-history.html.

32. *National Hispanic American Heritage Month,* n.d. http://www.hispanicheritagemonth.gov.

33. There's a common misconception that this is Mexican Independence Day, which is actually celebrated on September 16.

34. Taylor, López, Martinez, and Velasco, "When Labels Don't Fit: Hispanics and Their Views of Identity."

35. Alicia Menéndez, "My Gringa Mother. Tell Us Your Story. A Conversation about Identity." *Pew Hispanic Center,* n.d. http://www.pewhispanic.org/2012/06/01/alicia-menendez-my-gringa-mother/.

36. Weiner, *Discovering Successful Pathways in Children's Development.*

37. Richard Rodríguez, *Hunger of Memory: The Education of Richard Rodríguez.* Boston: D.R. Godine, 1982.

FOUR

Voces about Family

My inheritance comes in the form of family and love. What I have inher-
ited is a strong faith, a will to persevere, and desire to be inclusive, the
honor of hard work, and the beauty of my culture. It's an inheritance
money can't buy. It's priceless. My Latino inheritance guides me every
day of my life. It's made me who I am. It brings me hope and peace.[1]

The Latino family can be aptly compared with an anchor by virtue of
the dual and conflicting roles it plays in the life of children. On the one
hand, as affirmed by Lorena Garza González in the opening words of this
chapter, the family nurtures character strengths that are associated with
well-being and success and is a stabilizing force that helps children and
adults weather the turbulent process of immigration. At the same time,
some practices, attitudes, and circumstances associated with Latino families can create drag for children and adults, rendering it harder for them to
make headway in their adopted country.

Building on our discussion in Chapter 3 of the resources deployed by
Latino children to rise above adversity, the voices in this chapter provide
insight on how to unlock the power of the Latino family, along the lines sug-
gested by education experts Robert Rueda and Carmen DeNeve as follows:

Cultural diversity and the resulting disparity in student achievement
are not problems that will resolve themselves. As we prepare for the
many educational challenges of the next century, we must learn how
to build bridges between students' home cultures and the cultures of

their schools. These bridges are essential for student academic success, and without them, we do a serious disservice to both students and the larger society that will ultimately benefit from the development of their special talents. We encourage you as educators to draw on the bridge-building resources already at your fingertips—the funds of knowledge of your students, their families, and the paraeducators from your community.[2]

LATINO FAMILIES BY THE NUMBERS[3]

Household and Family Structure

11.6 million: Number of Latino family households in the United States in 2012

3.87:   Average size of Latino households in the United States (compared with 3.19 for all people)

65.7:   Percentage of Latino children under 18 who live with two married parents (compared with 64% of all American children under 18)

15:   Percentage of Latinos 16–25 years of age who are married (compared with 9% of all Americans in that age-group)

Household Economy

27:   Median age of Latinos (compared with 37 for the American population)

$38,624:   Median household income of U.S. Latinos (compared with $50,233 for American households)

25.3:   Percentage of U.S. Latinos living in poverty (compared with 14% of the American population)

46.1:   Percentage of U.S. Latinos who are homeowners (compared with 66.1% of all Americans)

Perspectives and Practices

77:   Percentage of Latino parents who think that going to college is the number-one priority for their kids after high school[4]

45:   Percentage of Latino high school students who report having had sexual intercourse (compared with 48% of all high school students)[5]

44:   Percentage Latinas who get pregnant at least once before age 20[6]

94:   Percentage of Latino teens who think it's important to be
                     told to abstain from sex until after high school[7]

Six core values are key to understanding Latino family life: *familismo,
cariño, machismo, marianismo, respeto,* and *educación.* The discussion that follows examines each of these, focusing on how they impact
Latino children, for better as well as for worse. Also important to
this discussion are seven character strengths that are known to correlate
with life satisfaction, academic success, and more broadly, high achievement, namely, grit, self-control, zest, social intelligence, gratitude, optimism, and resilience.[8] A key objective of this chapter is to explore how
Latino family life supports the development of these strengths as well as
those associated with resilience, as discussed in Chapter 3.

As always, it is important to remember that by necessity, discussions of
this nature entail making generalizations that may not hold across all U.S.
Latinos, but may actually vary along a wide range of variables, including
country of origin, socioeconomic background, level of acculturation to
American life, as well as individual differences.

We start our overview of the Latino family with a poem that previews
some of the main points of this chapter. Reuben Chavira's tribute to his
mom speaks to the strength of Latino mothers, the positive attributes of
marianismo, the power of resilience, and the central place of *cariño* in
family interactions.

A fourth-generation resident of La Puente, California, Reuben is studying psychology at Adams State University and wants to pursue graduate
studies in the field of social psychology to work with at-risk populations,
using poetry "as a mechanism for generating social emotions, establishing
a space for expression and creativity that can then be channeled toward
academic achievement." Reflecting on the role that poetry has played in
his own life, he writes: "Growing up in La Puente, poetry helped keep
me out of gangs and away from drugs. Life teaches without teaching, and
poetry helped me learn life's lessons without having to be directly taught
in a classroom. I would read poems about issues in my life that were significant to me, and the inspirational words would become a guide for me
when I felt lost. I hope that through my future graduate level work, and
through my direct involvement with the community, I can bring the same
sense of focus and belonging to others."

Reuben's words, along with those of other youth in this book, form the
basis of our suggestion in the "Afterword" that schools should post inspirational messages in Spanish and hold afterschool reading clubs as a way
to create an additive school experience.

Mamá

She's having a procedure
Purely precautionary
I tell her to stop eating rich people food
We're poor folk

And her body is starting to rebel.
She taught me to be a rebel
To speak with more bass than treble
To never run from trouble
So I stand tall while others tremble.

She's what my speech resembles
Why I speak poetry
Sequencing syllables into ensembles
The reason I reach for symbols to help me explain.

She's an icon for overcoming pain
Putting others before her own personal gain. . . .
Believes in magic, still
And taught me to talk to plants.

This was how she raised me
And why in school I was considered advanced
She showed me the world within words
And taught my soul to dance.

These poems
They sometimes put me in a trance
Something like a reminisce
Where I reform the things I miss
I'm reborn through this
Process of purification.

She's having a procedure tomorrow
And if I had some time to borrow
I would make her some arts and crafts
Make up jokes to make her laugh
I'd sit still for an hour
To show her I could
To show her she did good
Raising her trees to grow up to stand tall.

Some consider success
To be having money to lend
She taught me that truth is
It's the meanings impressed
Upon the time that we spend.

So I inject emotion into these words that I bend
Because passion is more than a fashion or trend
And if you ration the weight of your words
It'll change the way it's heard.

She taught me to be sincere
To be honest
These are the things that people will hear.

This is why I speak with more bass than treble
Why I never run from my troubles
Why I stand tall and don't tremble.

She's what my passions resemble.

She's having a procedure soon
And I can't stop thinking about the stars and the moon
Stuck in a trance
Reminiscing upon magic

> And talking to plants
>
> Letting my soul dance
>
> Just the way she taught me.

CORE VALUES OF LATINO FAMILY LIFE

Familismo: Family First

> I asked for permission to go to the World Cup, and they didn't allow
> me. . . . I had to think about it for two days with my family and kids
> and I made the decision to quit because I want to go to the World Cup
> and see my kid play. Work is secondary.[9]

> Look for your passion and follow it, come what may, but do it from
> a Latino perspective, where you are guided by the effect of what you
> do on your family and your community.[10]

These quotes speak to the essence of *familismo,* a core cultural value of
the Spanish-speaking world that is characterized by a strong orientation and
commitment toward the family. *Familismo* plays a particularly critical role
in the lives of U.S. Latinos, by virtue of its ability to provide much-needed
social capital and a safety net for those in need. It also promotes the development of key character strengths in children, such as optimism and gratitude,
and values, such as helping those in need and rejecting materialism.

The following speak to these functions of *familismo.* They also capture
a key difference between the Spanish-speaking cultures and mainstream
American culture with regard to who is considered family. While English
family typically refers to the nuclear family, the notion of *familia* encompasses the extended family over several generations, and even *padrinos*
(godparents) and very close friends.

1. My aunt and uncle were the type of people that helped everyone out.
   They had a small one-bedroom apartment, where they lived with their
   five children. Whenever any family members would come from Mexico, they would end up at their house. There would be people sleeping
   on the sofa and on the floor. The best thing is that everyone was happy.
   Although my aunt and uncle didn't have much money, they always had
   food and shelter for anyone that needed it.
2. There are four kids in my family; with my mom and dad, my grandmother and my mom's brother, that made eight. And although we lived

in a cramped two-bedroom apartment our doors were always open to others. My mom used to say: as long as we have beans, we'll have food to eat. The funny thing is that now that I live away from home I miss our full house. I miss my little brother's screams, the aroma of my mom's cooking, and my dad's football. The most important thing is family, not material possessions or the number of beds.

In keeping with *familismo,* Latino children are socialized to value cohesiveness and cooperation over individualism and to put the welfare of the family ahead of their own. Once considered an impediment to progress in American society, *familismo* has been shown to contribute to the well-being of Latino children. In one study, 10th and 12th graders who felt a high sense of obligation to help and support their families were also concerned with doing well in school and pursuing their education beyond the high school years.[11] In another study, Latino students singled out their future obligations to their parents as their primary rationale for striving toward educational and occupational achievement.[12] The following students echo similar sentiments:

1. Every time I feel like giving up my parents' words are the ones that keep me from breaking down. There are times in which I only get two hours of sleep. Sometimes all I have time to eat is one meal. Despite this I will not give up, I do not care if I have to pull all-nighters every day. I will graduate from college and earn a diploma, which my parents can be proud of. *Si no fuera por la familia* (if it were for family), I think I would have given up on school a long time ago.

2. I feel like I'm the only hope for my family sometimes. My parents are very proud that I am studying and I can't help the emotions I feel when I think about how my parents look at me with pride. They expect that I will find a job and take care of them. Sometimes I have doubts because of problems with my eyesight; the fear that one day, I may go completely blind. But I have to put these thoughts out of my mind and continue my studies with all the fight I have in me.

For all its strengths, *familismo* also has significant shortcomings—from burdening children with excessive obligations and stresses to undermining their academic goals. Older siblings, especially females, are particularly vulnerable, as they are often saddled with the care of younger siblings and other parental obligations. The following stories attest to these and other burdens. Just as important, they speak to the personal characteristics that help children bear these burdens, in particular, their gratitude and appreciation of the sacrifices made by others on their behalf, their keen understanding of the challenges they face, and their unbending commitment to making the best of their circumstances.

1. None of my Latino friends ever had the luxury of just going home and doing their homework. There was always other work that took priority. Whether it was the house that needed to be cleaned, the cooking that had to be done, the errands that had to be run, or, in my case, going to work with my stepfather. For a lot of Latin families, it's as if once their children graduate from high school they expect them to get a job and forget about school. At 16 I was already working at the mall and by the time I graduated from high school I was a manager at a store. My parents didn't quite understand at the time why I wanted to quit my job and continue my education by going to college because I was doing so well. My stepfather wanted me to continue working with him but once I explained the benefits of having an engineering background in working for a construction company, he began to see things the way I did.

2. This year, my father has had trouble finding work in construction. And so, he had to move to a nearby city. He stays there during the week and comes home on the weekends. Since we're a family of 7, I have had to step in to help. Some days I work as many as 10 hours. This is taking a toll on my schoolwork. When I get home I'm just too tired to study. I had to drop my math class because I fell behind and realized that I was going to flunk. My dad is very proud and he would never accept this if he weren't desperate.

3. When I was 10 my dad was sent to jail. Life became difficult then because my mom couldn't do everything by herself. My brother, who was 16, had to get a job and his grades started to slip. When we told my dad about this, he broke out crying because he realized what he had done to us. When my sister turned 16 she also got a job and gave my mom everything she made. I remember that she would go to my parent-teacher conferences because my mom was working. She would also pick me up from school every day and would take care of me when I was sick.

Cariño: An Ethos of Caring

The sense of affection, intimacy, and gratitude expressed in many of the comments in this chapter embodies the concept of *cariño,* a hallmark of

Latino family life. Parents and children hug and kiss often and call each other by terms of endearment, such as *nena* ("baby girl") or *m'hijo* (my child). While American teenagers may seek to distance themselves from their families and may shy away from displays of affection, Latino adolescents actually seek out *cariño*. In the following text, one young man's decision to opt out of celebrating his high school graduation with his peers in order to be with his family may strike non-Latinos as peculiar, if not abnormal, until seen through the prism of *familismo* and *cariño*. The same applies to the behavior of aunts and the grandmother, which can come across as possessive and selfish from an American perspective.

I was so happy to hear all the cheers of my family and friends at my high school graduation ceremony. After the ceremony, my aunt asked me if I wanted to go to Macaroni Grill to eat. I turned around and told my parents that I couldn't because I was going to Grad Night. My mom was upset saying they had been waiting to eat because they wanted to go out and celebrate with me. However, I had already bought my ticket and the bus was leaving in an hour. My mom seemed surprised and asked me what Grad Night was. I guess I forgot to tell them I was going. When I said that I would go to a specific place and stay there all night, my mom didn't understand why I was staying out all night. My aunts thought that Americans were boring for having such a celebration and they insisted I stay here with them and have a celebration with only family. I tried to explain to my family that I had already bought my ticket, but my grandmother said that if I didn't go with them she was going to be sick and it would all be my fault. My night ended with a belly full of Italian food and a movie with my family. Full belly, happy heart! It turned out to be a good night after all.

The sway of *cariño* spills over to other contexts, particularly school, where it has been shown to increase Latino children's engagement and contribute to additive schooling. In their study of Latino paraeducators (support services personnel such as instructional assistants and teacher aides), Robert Rueda and Carmen DeNeve describe school practices that align with an ethos of *cariño* and explain how these benefit Latino students.

The ideas and practices they use often seem to provide comfort zones for the students in learning and being motivated in the classroom. Sometimes these strategies are subtle, such as physical proximity to students or a hand on the shoulder at a strategic moment. Other times they are less subtle, such as the use of locally meaningful phrases, terms, or ideas that generate engagement and positive response from the children. For example, we noticed that paraeducators might often call their students *"mijo,"* which is an affectionate term often used by Latino parents, meaning "my little one."[13]

Machismo and Marianismo: A Code of Conduct for Men and Women

MACHISMO

Cast in its most negative light, machismo in the United States is associated with Latino men who are stereotyped as lazy, unfaithful, and abusive. However, *machismo,* in principle, holds men to a higher set of standards, including protecting and providing for their loved ones and being courageous, honorable, and selfless. The following fathers embody these virtues. Their stories paint a picture of Latino fathers, and Latino men in general, seldom noted, let alone appreciated, in mainstream American society.

1. I've never had to work to help my family, and I feel very lucky about that. My dad, who had to drop out of school to help his parents, did everything in his power to make sure that we did not have to do the same. My grandparents were very poor and could not afford to send my dad to school. But my dad loved school and was a very good student—so good, in fact, that that he got a scholarship. But knowing that his family needed him, my dad never told his parents about the scholarship and he dropped out of school so that he could work more. He's very proud that I will be graduating from college this year and that my sister has just completed her first year in Humboldt State University.

2. My father is a gardener. He's a legal resident but because he never got very far in school in Mexico he has no other option but to do this very difficult work. In the summer, the harsh sun beats down on him sucking every drop of water from his body. He works hard to do the best he can. The days are long but he only thinks about his family. He only thinks about making enough money to put food on the table for us. He would love to be able to offer us more, but he can't. All he can do is to make sure that his children never have to struggle so hard.

3. My dad has always been there for us. Throughout high school I would wake up not wanting to go to school. I remember that my dad would always lecture me on how important school was, how I needed to graduate from high school and go to college. He drove me to school

every single day during high school, which was a thirty-minute drive. The day of my graduation he was there, beaming with pride. And he's still supporting me. He tells me at the end all my work will pay off. I see how hard life is without an education. My dad works 365 days a year. If he doesn't go to work he doesn't get paid. I want to have a better life than what he has had. He taught me to strive for more and have big dreams.

MARIANISMO

Who is Gloria Estefan today? I'm very fulfilled as a woman. I've been able to have a wonderful family life, a fantastic career. I have a lot of good friends around me. My family has been my grounding point, and rooted me deeply to the earth. . . . I'm very happy. I've done everything I ever wanted to do. The key to me was—I told my husband when we were in our 20s—I'm going to work really hard, so one day I won't have to work so hard. And to me what that was, was having choices. And I do have choices now—and I have taken full advantage of that. It's important for me now to be here for my little girl [Emily, age 12]. My son is full grown—and I know how quickly that goes. So, I'm balancing being a mother—which to me is the most important role I have on this earth—and still being creative, writing—which is what I love to do.[14]

The counterpart to *machismo* is *marianismo,* a concept originating in Catholicism, which holds that the Virgin Mary embodies all of the virtues of womanhood, in particular, selflessness, humility, passivity, honor, and purity of body and soul and that defines the female role as being mothers, caregivers, and nurturers.[15] Seldom noted, but equally pertinent to a discussion of Latina gender roles are characteristics such as resolve, strength, and courage. The latter are associated with *hembrismo* (literally "femaleness"), a term that researchers Alberta Gloria and Theresa A. Segura-Herrera colorfully describe as connoting a "Chicana version of Superwoman, who is expected to proficiently fulfill multiple roles both in and out of the home."[16] Mother, singer, songwriter, actress, and entrepreneur Gloria Estefan, cited at the top of this section, exemplifies a Cuban version of Superwoman. Lesser known, but no less impressive, are the Chicana Superwomen featured in the following texts:

1. During the day she's mami, but at night she's Julia Pérez. Two very different people in the same body. With pain in her bad leg, she drags herself out of bed and goes to the back room to take care of her baby

grandson. She then drives my dad to work and returns home to clean, cook, and take care of her grandson. As the sun sets, it's time for school. She always sits in the back because she's embarrassed of her leg or her tired looks from too many all-nighters. She speaks softly, so that her classmates won't notice her accent. Returning home, she asks her daughters for help. Can they check her email to her professor to make sure that it sounds okay? After all these years, she's still insecure about her English. She looks at the dinner table that she will have to clear, her books scattered among the dirty plates and our leftovers. Her life unfolds on this table.

2. "*Magaly ya levántate para ir al escuela*" (Magaly, get up already to go to school) says my mom on a regular Monday morning. I can smell pancakes from my room. As I try to get my head together, all I hear is chaos around the house because we all seem to be running late. '*¡Apúrate Magaly que ya me voy en 20 minutos, se queda el que se queda!*' (hurry up, Magaly. I'm leaving in 20 minutes, whoever falls behind stays behind). As I walk into the kitchen I see three lunches ready in the table ready to be put in everyone's *mochilas* (backpack). As I hurry my two younger sisters are finishing getting ready and I pay attention to my mom who has waken up *a las 5 de la madrugada* (5 A.M.) to shower, make breakfast, and still prepare our lunches. My mom is from Minatitlán, Veracruz and came to the U.S. when she was 20. She came using my *tía's* papers. She found a job in a factory, but my mom *se puso las pilas* (got smart) and enrolled in school. She graduated from Compton Community College and forced my dad to finish his high school. She divorced my dad when I was 12 and stayed with us four- my oldest brother, my 2 younger sisters, and me. I think to myself how does she do it? In 2009 my mom went back to school to improve her *inglés* and maybe she would get the promotion where she works as a school library assistant. Her day has always been waking up early, taking us to different schools, going to work, picking us up, going to night school, and getting home and cooking for the next day. *Esta mujer estaba llena de energía para ser un éxito y no quería que nada nos faltara.* (This woman was full of energy to be a success and did not want us to go without). I like to call her superwoman. Today she is very proud of me, not only for being the first to attend a university, but also for being the first girl to be the closest to "making it." She has given me the knowledge and importance of what it is to be Latina and not to depend on anyone, *me enseñó que si quiero algo, pues nada viene fácil y a trabajar para alcanzar las estrellas* (she taught me that

if I want something, it's never going to come easy and to work to reach the stars). Thanks to *la Virgencita* who has looked over us and has given us all the strength we need. *¡Gracias mamá por ser la mamá mas mejor del mundo!* (Thanks, mom for being the best mom in the world).

Like the stories of fathers cited earlier, these accounts give lie to simplistic notions surrounding Latino gender roles. Images of passive and submissive women with no other ambition in life than to serve their families give way to more complex realities, where the right combination of *marianismo* and *hembrismo* actually prove essential to the success of immigrant children.

Notwithstanding these positives, it would be misleading—not mention counterproductive to this discussion—to suggest that Latino beliefs and practices surrounding gender roles and sexuality pose no negatives. One area where such negatives loom large is teenage sexuality. Though Latino high school students are just as likely to be sexually active as their non-Latino peers, their pregnancy and childbirth rates are nearly twice as high as the national average. Life altering and long lasting, the consequences of teenage childbearing include low educational attainment, depression, poverty, and higher rates of incarceration, for the teen parents, as well as their children.[17]

Beliefs and behavior premised on the worst of *familismo,* machismo and *marianismo* play a significant role in this state of affairs. Chief among these is the notion that marriage and motherhood are the essence of womanhood and are incompatible with getting an education and pursuing a career. Another major factor is the fact that sexuality is a taboo subject in many Latino homes, which is a reason why Latino teens feel they need more information on this topic.[18] The following story, reproduced from Chapter 3, points to another consideration: the wide gap between traditional Latino parents and their acculturated children surrounding matters of sexuality. More generally, this remarkable account speaks to how immigration compounds intergenerational differences, as children are exposed to belief systems in the new country that are radically different from those of their parents.

Latino parents often want to impose on their children the values and practices that their parents imposed on them. They are particularly strict with their daughters. I love my parents, but I wish they would be a little more approving of my decisions. I try to explain to my mom that things are different here, but she doesn't understand. I remember when I decided to risk it and tell my mom that I wanted to move in with my boyfriend of five years. I didn't know exactly how she was going to react, but I had a hunch that it wouldn't be well. Sure enough, she waited for a minute or two and then said: Oh no, not before marriage.

Deep inside I feared that my mom would never think of me the same way. We feel very differently about so many things, and this is one of them. After seeing the fear and sadness on her face, I nervously tried to explain to her why I wanted to live with my boyfriend. I told her that I wanted to live with him because I wanted to know what it was like to be around him all the time. I explain that I didn't want to rush into marriage and being so young, that I didn't feel that it was a good idea for us to get married yet. With every sentence I said, she became more confused and sad. I told her that I didn't understand why this hurt her so much. I explained that things are different in this country and in my generation. I said that I knew people that had lived together before getting married who went on to have a wonderful marriage. I told her that I loved him and trusted him very much. I added that he and I were very responsible and mature, that we had known each other for a long time, and that we were serious about marriage in the future and wanted to prepare for it.

But my mom didn't budge. She said: it would make me much happier if you married him before living with him. She reasoned that since we had already been together for so long we should go ahead and get married. She said that my father would have a hard time accepting this and added that she had heard of couples who had broken up after moving in together. I told her that this wouldn't happen to us and I explained that I wanted to get my degree before getting married.

Eventually, I had no choice but to point out that as an adult I was entitled to make my own decisions. I love and respect my parents but I believe that living with him before marriage is in my best interest. Sometimes Latin parents don't allow their children to grow. They restrict their freedom only because of old customs and beliefs that they learned as children.

For all the criticism leveled by youth against old customs and beliefs, some Latino customs and beliefs are known to promote healthy family interactions and protect children against negative influences, including sexual risk behavior. Indeed, one of the most common reasons that sex education programs directed at Latino youth fail to achieve their intended results is they do not strike the right cultural chord. At best, such programs fail to leverage the strengths of familism, machismo, and *marianismo*. At worse, they are outright hostile to them, viewing them as antithetical to achieving success and personal fulfillment in American society.[19]

By contrast, the following practices of pregnancy prevention programs are known to be particularly effective: being respectful of Latino values and behavior surrounding gender roles and sexuality; involving male partners as well as family members, having Spanish-speaking mentors with intercultural skills; fostering self-esteem and high expectations; providing financial incentives for college; and inviting Latino guest speakers to discuss career opportunities with youth.[20]

One young woman's experience calls attention to another important practice: teaching youth to rise above common negative stereotypes and diminished expectations surrounding Latino youth.

> My parents work long hours and don't have time to go shopping. One day, my dad dropped me off with my little brother and sister at a store and asked me to buy them shoes. My little sister, who was 2 years old at the time, was difficult to deal with. She kept running around the store and pulling things off the shelves. When it was time to pay, the cashier looked at me and said: how old is she? When I answered, she gave me a sad look and told me that she would give me a special discount. I was so happy about saving my parents money that I didn't ask myself why she had done this. It was only after I told my mom that I realized that the cashier thought I was a teenage mother and felt sorry for me. She assumed something about me that wasn't true. Well, over time I proved that cashier wrong and didn't become a Latina statistic—young and pregnant.

Perhaps surprisingly, these kinds of experiences with gender stereotypes are fairly common, even in places as unexpected as the school context. A study notes:

> Our respondents told us stories that illustrated how the intersection of ethnicity and gender create enhanced barriers for them. Girls in one of our focus groups, for example, reported that a non-Latino teacher in the school asked a ninth grade Latina student sitting with her friends in the cafeteria: "Why aren't you pregnant yet?" One of the girls we interviewed who was the oldest of several siblings and

often shouldered parenting duties, stated: "I have a lot of people tell me 'you're going to end up pregnant.'"[21]

The study warns that young women can come to internalize societal expectations, and it underscores the importance of attending to cultural values and showcasing successful Latinas. However, somewhat undermining this point, the study points to the general "absence of female role models or inspiring influences" as an obstacle to implementing such programs. We believe that this is a valid point insofar as it applies to Latina professionals, who are in relatively short supply in American society. However, it is not valid as it applies to Latinas in general, as the stories of strong, resourceful, selfless, and enterprising women in this chapter amply demonstrate. Though many of these women do not have prestigious careers, they are role models and inspiring influences, by virtue of how they comport themselves in their everyday lives.

This distinction, though seemingly trivial, actually bears on an important difference between American and Latino cultural values taken up next.

Respeto: The Recognition of the Dignity of the Individual

Though outwardly similar, Spanish *respeto* and English "respect" actually differ from each other in subtle but important ways. University of New Mexico Professor Patricia Covarrubias has studied these terms as they pertain to Americans and Mexicans. According to her, for Americans, respect has to be earned and is linked with "fair play and democratic spirit," while for Mexicans, *respeto* "is not a social benefit one has to earn . . . but is conferred upon persons on the basis of who they are more than what they do."[22] In our experience, this holds true for other Latino nationalities as well.

Rosa María Jiménez, featured also in Chapter 2, captures this difference in a prizewinning essay that she wrote as an undergraduate at the University of California at Davis:

If I say "*Respeto* a mis padres . . . I always will," I do not mean the same thing as my white friend Susan does when she says "I respect my parents . . . I always will." I mean that I respect my parents and their authority in a country where they have suffered humiliation, poverty, and disrespect. In contrast, Susan may mean that she respects her parents because they are doctors. In English "respect" has become a cultural formality, while in Spanish *respeto* is loaded with deep cultural meaning.[23]

Coming back to the earlier discussion surrounding best practices for Latino youth, Rosa María's comment speaks to the need to expand the concept of "role models and inspirational figures" to include mothers and fathers such as those featured earlier, whose way of being exemplify the notion of *respeto* and illustrate the value of grit, gratitude, optimism, self-control, and so on. Given Latino cultural values, these individuals are as inspirational and, more to the point, as important to the future of Latino youth as any accomplished professional or public figure.

Buena Educación: Moral, Social, and Personal Responsibility

Like *respeto,* Spanish *educación* deviates from its English look-alike in significant ways. Latino men, women, and children are all bound by the code of *buena educación* (good education), which entails treating elders with respect, being considerate of others, having social graces, and being morally upstanding. Furthermore, as captured in a colorful anecdote by Puerto Rican linguist Ana Celia Zentella, *educación* is also about having common sense and being an original thinker.

> Whenever teachers told *mami* I had a high IQ, she would rephrase that concept in her inimitable way: "Yes," she would say, "she has plenty of ICE CUBES, but they are melting in her brain because she has no common sense. *Mami* distrusted IQ scores and book learning and favored common sense and creativity, especially being, as she pronounced it, "oriyinal" (original). All her life, if I happened to say something she considered on target or insightful, she would demand: *"¿Eso es tuyo, o te lo leíste en algún libro?"* (Is that your own [idea] or did you read it in a book?). It just didn't count as much if it wasn't "original."[24]

To those unfamiliar with the concept of *educación,* comments such as this might signal a disregard, if not outright contempt for schooling on the part of Latino parents. In fact, because the notion of *educación* serves as the foundation for all learning and includes moral, social, and personal responsibility, it is critical to improving academic outcomes for U.S. Latinos. Angela Valenzuela (cited in Chapter 1 in the context of describing subtractive school) explains the importance of *educación* in the school context as follows: "When teachers deny their students the opportunity to engage in reciprocal relationships, they simultaneously invalidate the definition of education that most of these young people embrace . . . Lost to schools is an opportunity to foster academic achievement by building on the strong motivational force embedded in students' familial identities."[25]

Of course, many Latino parents also endorse practices and perspectives associated with English *education*. Some, such as those featured as follows, resort to extraordinary measures to ensure their children succeed in school:

1. My parents themselves never completed grammar school, but they understood the opportunity that was given to us in the United States. They wanted their six children to have a better quality of life than they had as farm workers in the San Joaquin Valley (in Central California) so they figured out a way to motivate us to stay in school and take advantage of the opportunities they never had. That motivation came every summer when they would take us to *la tabla* in the hot vineyards of the Valley. We would have to pick grapes and put them on a sheet of paper in between the rows so that they could dry and become raisins. My five sisters and I absolutely hated this, but every time we complained my parents simply said, "If you don't get an education this is what you're going to be doing for the rest of your life." The thought of waking up at 4:30 every day and working ten hours under that scorching sun was all the motivation we needed. When it came time for us to think about college, they had to depend on our high school to guide us through the colossal task that was the application process. Thankfully, our high school had a program for students like us. Educators should realize that there are many Latino parents out there who care and want their children to succeed. All they need is a little help along the way.

2. When I was seven years old, I began to have trouble with English. Language had not been an issue 'til I began to have problems interacting with my classmates and teachers at school. Insecurity and intimidation became a recurring feeling when I would enter class. I found myself not being able to speak, write or understand what I was hearing and seeing in class. The school sent my parents a letter stating that I needed to attend classes for two hours after school until my situation improved. This caused my parents great worry and concern. As the school year came to an end and summer approached, I began to feel great relief.

But my relief soon turned to anger when my parents informed me that I would have to live and breathe English for the summer months. My older sister, who was fluent in English, was going to be my teacher. Every day, for five hours, I had to write, read, and speak English. I would get angry, sad, and frustrated to the point that I would cry. I hated how I could not be playing and enjoying my summer like the rest of my classmates. My parents constantly reminded me how one day I would be thankful. When school started again I had become such an expert in English that there was no evidence that I had ever had problems. For the first time, I felt like a student should feel on the first day of school, excited about the future and happy to be around other children.

3. After only one week in school, I decided I couldn't take it any more and I resolved never to return. When I got home, I told my mom about my decision. To my great surprise, she wasn't bothered or alarmed. She only said that English also caused her a great deal of problems. When Monday arrived, I woke up calm and convinced that I would never again have to return to school. However, before I could get out my bed, my mom entered my room with a smoothie and a change of clothes. At this moment, I realized what was happening and I began to cry. But my mom had not failed me. Yes, I had to return to school, but I would not return alone. As usual, she took me by the hand until we reached the classroom door and gave me a kiss right before the bell rang. But that day, she didn't turn around to go home. Instead, she came into the class, put her purse on the teacher's desk, and got comfortable in the back of the room in between a mountain of boxes. My mom spent the whole morning sharpening pencils, dusting bookshelves, and organizing books. That whole school year she worked as a volunteer, offering help wherever needed. At the end of the year, the two of us had learned quite a bit of English and she had become everyone's favorite mom. When I began first grade, I wasn't afraid of anything or anyone.

If there were an award for most shrewd and resourceful parenting, these parents would surely be strong contenders for it. Unfortunately, they are the exception more than the rule. The fact is that despite their good intentions and considerable cultural resources, many Latino parents are unable to help their children with the demands of school due to a wide range of limitations, including unfamiliarity with the American system of education, language barriers, heavy work demands, and a lack of education. These limitations are explored in the sections that follow.

HEADWINDS AND DESTABILIZING FORCES
OF IMMIGRATION

Some of the most powerful forces that threaten the stability of Latino families are not directly connected to cultural values, but are related to immigration. The pervasiveness and severity of the many problems associated with immigration are on display throughout this book. Less visible, but no less real, is the emotional and psychological toll that these strains and stresses can take on children. In his book *How Children Succeed,* Paul Tough discusses some emerging findings that bear on this issue:

> The part of the brain most affected by stress is the prefrontal cortex, which is critical in self-regulatory activities of all kinds, both emotional and cognitive. As a result, children who grow up in stressful environments generally find it harder to concentrate, harder to sit still, harder to rebound from disappointments, and harder to follow directions. . . . Some of the effects of stress on the prefrontal cortex can best be categorized as emotional or psychological: anxiety and depression of all kinds.[26]

Confounding expectations, however, studies indicate that immigrant Latino youths actually have a better behavior and achievement profile than would be expected from their circumstances. In particular, they have lower rates of alcohol consumption, fewer behavioral problems, and more positive academic attitudes and behavior than their nonimmigrant peers.[27] Latino immigrants, in general, also have a health advantage over non-Latinos, as well as Latinos born in the United States including significantly higher survival rates for many medical conditions, including heart disease, cancer, and diabetes, and they live longer than non-Hispanic whites.

Though the causes behind this so-called Hispanic paradox are not yet fully understood, it is believed that traditional Latino cultural values and practices may have a hand in some of the positive outcomes. For Latino children, family values, religious involvement, and negotiating a bicultural identity are believed to be particularly valuable.[28]

The discussion that follows takes inventory of the stresses that immigration places on Latino families. In the process, it also captures some of the mechanisms at work behind the Hispanic paradox.

NAVIGATING WITHOUT A MAP OF EXPERIENCE

The backdrop to many of the stories in this chapter is a phenomenon that affects many immigrant families, whereby the roles of the children and the adults are reversed. Psychologists Marcelo and Carola Suárez Orozco describe this phenomenon as follows: "In all societies, a critical role of parents is to act as guides for their children. Immigration undermines this function by removing the 'map of experience' necessary to competently escort the children in the new culture. Without effortless proficiency in the new culture, immigrant parents are less able to provide guidance in negotiating the currents of a complex society; they must also rely on their children for cultural explanations."[29]

In keeping with this, in the situations that follow, it is the children who contend with complicated financial issues, handle difficult conversations, teach and protect the adults, provide and care for the family, and fend for themselves. The sheer number of stories of this type shared by our students underscores just how widespread and dominant these experiences are in the lives of Latino youths. Difficult and stressful as these experiences are, however, it should come as no surprise that they also promote social competence and positive psychological outcomes in children by pushing them to develop valuable skills and by instilling in them a sense of self-sufficiency and agency.[30]

Contending with Complicated Financial Issues

Once I was at the bank with my mom and the person who was helping her asked for the account number for our home loan. My mom signaled for me to take over. When I gave the bank employee the information, he looked at me in disbelief. I was only 11 years old and knew all the details of our loan. As I think about it now, it seems strange that I would know all of this.

Handling Difficult Conversations

1. When I was 7 years old I used to accompany my dad to help him look for more work as a gardener. I remember we would go to rich people's homes and ask them if they needed us to clean their patios. My dad understood a little English, but he didn't speak it well. My dad decided to send me out, telling me what to say and how much to ask for. For one year, I was the one that to go out and try and find him work.

2. I have always understood the need to help my parents when they try to communicate with people. I remember an occasion when I took my mom to the doctor. During the 15-minute consultation, the doctor and I were practically the only ones speaking. I knew the medication and

the dosage she was taking by heart and I was able to communicate that to the doctor without having to ask my mom. At one point during the visit, I turned around and saw my mom, sitting there quietly and feeling a bit sorry for me, and then it hit me what she must have been feeling. I think she felt out of place that the roles had been reversed. I was taking on the role of the "adult" and she the one of dependent. After thinking about it for a while, I promised myself that from now on I would always turn around and look at my mom during my conversations in English and be sure that I always take her into account and ask her opinion.

3. When I was in fifth grade I had just moved to a new school and a boy began to pick on me. I was very upset and when I told my mom she said she would talk to the teacher about it. I went with her to the meeting and I ended up having to do all of the talking because my mom did not speak English. In the end, the conference didn't help but at least it showed the teachers that my parents were aware of what was going on and cared. At the time I felt like it was pointless and even discouraged my parents to go because I knew that I would end up doing all of the work.

Protecting and Teaching the Adults

1. I love my mom very much and can't bear it when someone mistreats her. I have had to defend her many times. One time in particular she accidentally hit another car while parking her car. The woman in the other car got out and started calling her a dumb Mexican and told her that if she didn't know how to drive she had no business driving. I told her to stop calling her Mexican and stupid, since she was neither of those things. But she wouldn't stop. She screamed louder and louder. So I started to swear. My mom got very scared and started to cry. I was only fourteen but I told her that I would always be there to defend her. To this day, whenever she needs me, I'm there for her.

2. I must have been about 14. My grandma asked me to go with her to the doctor's office. She said that whenever she went alone the nurses didn't treat her very well. She also needed me because she didn't know how to read or write. I noticed right away that the nurse was rude with us. She yelled at my grandma for her high blood pressure. All my grandma could do was look down in shame. I stepped in to defend her and told the nurse that that was no way to treat patients, especially older ones. When I complained to the doctor he said the nurse was probably having a rough day.

I said that I didn't think it was the problem but that regardless of the reason, it was not an acceptable or professional way to behave.

3. I was about ten years old and had just gotten home from school. I could hear my dad on the phone speaking to a collection's agent. My father understood English well but he had a hard time speaking it. By his tone of voice I could tell he was angry and he just kept repeating the same sentence over and over again, saying he didn't owe them anything. The person on the line was asking my father to give him his bank account number so that they could take out a certain amount of money every month. My dad was so frustrated that he handed me the phone. I told him that we did not think we owed them anything but if they showed us the bill we would pay. He said that they had mailed the bill but had been returned to sender. At the end, the man on the phone just said that I was wasting his time and hung up on me. We never heard back about this.

4. At age 13 my mother would ask me to tutor her in English, so I would spend many summers teaching my mom what I knew. To this day her English is not perfect, but so close to it. I am so glad and proud that she accomplished her goals and that I was a part of it.

Providing for the Family and Serving as Caregivers

1. My mother always tells me not to stress out, but she doesn't understand that I must work because she doesn't have enough money to support me and give me the opportunities to get ahead. Hispanic families are unlike the average American family: they depend on their children to help out.

2. During my last year of high school, I remember that my mom used to work a lot and was unable to go to conferences because her feet were hurting. During this time, my older sister would take me to school and would give me money for food. She was in charge of me during that year and for that reason I feel a stronger connection to her in comparison with my other siblings. She took care of me when I was sick. I would call her because my mom worked so much, she never answered the phone.

Fending for Themselves

1. My parents only have a 2nd grade education. Unlike an American child, I did not have highly educated parents to seek help from in case

I did not understand something from school. I could not ask for help with math because my parents didn't have the knowledge and I couldn't learn English from them because they did not speak it. In a way, this actually helped me because it forced me to learn things on my own without having to depend on them. I am not ashamed of my parents, but only wish that they had been fortunate enough to receive an education like the one I have.

2. My college counselor said to me "if you're the only one from your home to go to the university, your parents should make more sacrifices so that you won't have to work." That comment showed me that she had no idea of what being Hispanic is like. So many things went through my mind; like, we're a family of seven and my parents are already sacrificing so much. Also, they have never asked me to contribute to the rent or food. That's a big help. If I lived in an apartment or a dorm I couldn't make ends meet. For many Hispanics having a full time job is the only way to get through school.

Language Brokering

The challenges and rewards of language brokering have been discussed in Chapter 2. Here we revisit them briefly in the context of examining the reversal of roles connected with immigration.

Few roles assumed by immigrant children are as demanding as language brokering. Few are also as critically important to the well-being of the family. As discussed in Chapter 2, children hold conflicting views of language brokering, from feeling burdened by the responsibilities and fearful of making costly mistakes to deriving great satisfaction from being able to contribute to the well-being of their family. The following accounts recall earlier examples of children handling difficult, high-stakes transactions. Though they dwell primarily on the stresses associated with language brokering, it's easy to imagine how these types of experiences can also enhance children's sense of competence and social efficacy.[31]

1. October 14, a very happy day, my family was ready for my mom's appointment with immigration services. It's the day in which the immigration officer will determine if my mother can receive her residency of the United States. With frayed nerves and a bit of fear, we arrived at the office and turned in our appointment card. As we were sitting in the waiting room, an officer approached us and took us in a room where, before sitting down, asked my parents if they had brought a translator

with them. Immediately they said I was their translator. When I heard that I didn't know to do. I didn't want to make a mistake. The immigration officer began to ask questions in English I would translate them in Spanish to my parents. I was very nervous for fear that I may have forgotten some of the words in Spanish. When we had gone over all the questions, the officer looked at us and wouldn't say anything. The officer paused and said, "Sra. Flores," and he paused as we waited with anxiety. Then he said, "Welcome to the United States, You have just received your residency." In that moment we were relieved. I felt really good that I did not mess up my translation.

2. I remember a time when I was in fourth grade. It was parent-teacher conference week. It was four years that my father had been coming to this conference and he dreaded it because his English was not very good. He said he would always have problems communicating with the teachers and he would walk away with no idea on how I was doing in school. So one year they had the conference right after I got out of school. I had to sit out in the hall while he and my teacher spoke. Five minutes into the conference my dad comes out and says, "*mija, me tienes que ayudar. No entiendo nada de lo que me está diciendo* (Sweetie, you have to help me. I don't understand anything she is saying to me.)." I didn't know whether I could go in or not and I sort of felt embarrassed and sorry for my dad. I walked in and my teacher was smiling. She said it was great that I would do this and hoped that I would be truthful. I told him what my teacher was telling me. I was a really good student so I was really telling him the truth. Now my father and I laugh about it since now he speaks very good English. That day we made sure he would learn English for next year's conference. And he sure did!

3. When we were growing up, my brother, sister, and I always had to go with my parents everywhere just in case they needed someone to speak English. All three of us had to sit through bank, car, and house deals, etc. to explain everything detail by detail. This was sometimes scary to because if we had translated a certain thing the wrong way, we could have caused our parents to sign for a bad deal.

LOSING SOCIAL STATUS

Most immigrant parents struggle with feelings of inadequacy as they find themselves unable to guide their children in the new culture. Well-educated professionals in their home country face an added difficulty:

loss of social status. Unable to find employment in their field due to language barriers or legal status, they may have to resign themselves to doing menial work and not receiving the same amount of respect they are accustomed to receiving as professionals in their country of origin. The 2009 animated film *Cloudy with a Chance of Meatballs* takes a comedic approach to this situation. The character Manny (voiced by Latino actor Benjamin Bratt) is a cameraman for a weather network, but eventually it is revealed that he was actually a doctor in his native Guatemala.

In Southern California alone, there may be as many as 3,000 individuals like Manny, working mostly in construction, cleaning houses, or fast-food chains. A program at UCLA seeks to address the shortage of primary care doctors in California by tapping into these immigrants. The program offers them preparation classes for the medical board exams, mentorship from UCLA doctors, and financial support in exchange for their commitment to work for three years in underserved areas such as Riverside County, which has one primary care physician for every 9,000 residents.[32] In this way, program participants not only change their lives for the better but also effect positive change in the lives of others.

Unfortunately, programs such as these are few and far between. Without access to the opportunities afforded by such programs, most professionals who immigrate to this country resign themselves to doing jobs that don't take advantage of their skills and training. This common scenario is described next:

1. I am the daughter of two Salvadorian parents, who, like other Hispanics, came to this country for the "good life." They did not expect the things they have encountered. My mother was a nurse in El Salvador as well as a business person. Coming here not knowing any English, she immediately felt she was inferior to others. As my father says: "sure, it's nice being here and we have a good life, but if I had known that that people would be so judgmental, we would have never come here." My father felt embarrassed because he knew that he was being made fun of and was being judged for not speaking English very well. He struggled so long to try to speak it correctly. I, on the other hand, learned it quickly. "I read a book by Ana Castillo (*Sapagonia*). In the story, the main character says something that defines my feelings and those of my parents: In my country, I sound like the educated person that I am, but here, I am just the bus boy."

2. My mom delivers newspapers for a living. She gets up at 2:30 so that she can be done with her route by 6:30. I help her out on weekends and so does my boyfriend. We deliver a total of 400 newspapers. My mom's

friend, who also delivers newspapers, has a college degree from her home country but here she can only do this work. It's sad to see how much she struggles.

CRUSHING POVERTY

Poverty has wide ranging and, often, lifelong consequences for children, including negative health outcomes, instability of residence, inadequate nutrition, and, as discussed in Chapter 1, diminished academic outcomes. Immigrant Latino children, in particular, are among the hardest hit, being, at once more likely to live in poverty, as well as less likely to receive social services than their native-born counterparts. For all its challenges, however, poverty should never be associated with poor parenting practices or unhappy children. Indeed, studies of low-income parents show that many are affectionate, attentive to their children's success in school, and concerned for their safety and well-being.[33]

By the same token, affluence does not guarantee parenting success or fulfilled children. As psychologist Madeline Levine writes in her book *The Price of Privilege*: "America's newly identified at-risk group is pre-teen and teens from affluent, well-educated families. In spite of their economic and social advantages, they experience among the highest rates of depression, substance abuse, anxiety disorders, somatic complaints, and unhappiness of any group of children in this country." Some of the factors associated with this situation are isolation from parents and poor values, such as materialism, and endorsement of rule breaking and substance abuse. Conversely, emotional closeness to parents, self-efficacy (the belief in personal capability), and agency (the ability to act on one's behalf) are associated with positive outcomes for children. These qualities abound in the following families, making life more bearable in the face of crushing poverty and injecting hope for the future:

1. Work, money worries, and personal problems were always first with my parents. There was never any time for Open House or even for checking the grade book. My parents never understood or even tried to understand what it took to get into college. In my life the thing I've wanted most was that my parents get excited about my accomplishments. I always wanted them to be more involved, but it was never like that. With time, I have come to accept their way of being and I have come to understand that their background has a lot to do with it. Today I take comfort in knowing that they helped me by giving me a loving

family, a roof over my head, a table with food and the things I needed for school. But their greatest contribution was the opportunity to get an education. They understood that it was only by coming to this country they would make that possible.

2. I never suffered all that much because of poverty. But my sister did, because she was seven years older than me. I only remember two times when I felt poor. One of them was when my parents didn't have money to buy me a birthday present or even a cake. Around the time of my birthday we went to a birthday party for a co-worker of my dad's. My parents took a big piece of his birthday cake home and put a candle on it and sang happy birthday to me. The other incident was when my parents bought their home. We couldn't move in for a while because they needed to rent it. I had been wanting a dog for a long time and my dad said that when we moved into the house I would be able to have a dog. For many months I saved my lunch money preparing to buy a dog. Eventually I had $30, but before I had the chance to get my dog, I had to give it to my parents so that they could pay their bills.

Character strengths such grit, self-control, and optimism help the following youths cope with absolute poverty, as does the strategy of viewing their hardships from a perspective that diminishes their magnitude and gives them a higher meaning. As depicted in the following first comment, they may remind themselves of where they come from and where they are going. Alternatively, they may compare themselves with less fortunate people, as in the second comment, or, as in the last comment, they may avoid unfavorable comparisons and seek out peers who understand their hardships firsthand.

1. We arrived in this country without a lot of money and my parents had trouble finding a steady job. It was very difficult to have a stable life but I always understood why we had to move a lot. I was nervous when I enrolled in a new school and felt in my heart that nobody in this new place loved me. I was sad when my parents had to start over again, even if I didn't want to. But I thank God for giving me parents who were always there for me, attending to my needs. The sacrifices they made serve as a reminder of where I come from.

2. My family moved a lot because my dad was getting better jobs. We lived in 5 houses growing up. The children are the ones who suffer the most by the constant moving around. But that's the price to pay for the American dream, for making it here. As my dad says, all sacrifices

come with benefits. I know families who lived in one room for many years. It's difficult to live that way, with no privacy. No other group will sacrifice as much for the family as Latinos. Family is the most important thing for us and it will always be that way.

3. I once had a friend who was an only child and got everything she wanted. One day she invited me to a sleep over. When I saw her home I couldn't believe it. It was beautiful with big rugs, something I've never had in my life. Her backyard was ten times bigger and more beautiful than ours and it had so many toys. The next week, she asked me if she could have a sleep over at my house. Immediately I thought about our ugly floors, which look dirty and worn out no matter how hard my mom scrubs them. I told her that we lived very far away and that it wouldn't work out. I think she didn't believe me because eventually she became friends with other girls who lived in fancy houses. At first, I felt really bad but eventually I made new friends with girls in my neighborhood who knew what it was like to be poor.

FAMILY SEPARATION: A HEART DIVIDED

It is estimated that up to 80 percent of immigrant Latino children in U.S. schools are separated from their parents some time during their childhood as a result of immigration. For many children, separation creates feeling of isolation, loneliness, and sadness. In extreme cases, prolonged separations can lead children to reject their biological parents and view their caregivers in the United States as their legitimate parents.[34]

In a study of the impact of immigration on parent–child relationships, a Latino parent separated from his children movingly described this experience as a "heart divided."[35] The following youths describe similar heartbreaking experiences. But they do more than that. Remarkably, making use of critical strategies, they also take inventory of the higher goals that drive their separation from loved ones and summon gratitude and optimism. In so doing, they exemplify resilience.

1. I came to the U.S. in 1999 with my dad but my mom had to stay behind in Colombia. Even though we were going to be far away from each other, she insisted I go to study and become something in life. My parents provided me with a lot of support and they never denied me the opportunity to continue my education. But the hardest thing for me is that my mom was not able to share such beautiful moments with me, such as my high school graduation or visiting me at college.

2. My uncle came here from El Salvador but left his wife and three daughters behind. He came because he needed money and he knew going to Los Angeles was his only option. He missed his family a lot and hoped that he could return to El Salvador one day.

3. As long as I can remember, I've heard Americans say that immigrants are a burden who come here to take advantage of the system. But the reality is that most immigrants don't come here to take advantage of anything or to take anything away from anyone. On the contrary, they come feeling the pain of leaving loved ones behind. They come here to work hard to make a little money, just enough to send some back home and make ends meet here.

4. I once dated a guy who was born in Mexico and came to the United States to work when he was 14 years old. He left his mom and three little sisters behind. He was only able to talk to them once a week. He always said that although it was very hard to be so far away from them, it was best because he was able to send them money so they could live a little bit better.

THE DARK CLOUD OF DEPORTATION

Highly charged public discussions about immigration often obscure the human side of this issue, particularly the toll that the cloud of deportation takes on families and children. Keenly aware that their lives may be uprooted at any time due to their immigration status, many Latino children live in a state of fear and hypervigilance, and suffer from separation anxiety. Deportation—the threat of it, let alone the actual experience of it—is highly traumatic for Latino children and is associated with a wide range of negative outcomes, including academic problems, sadness, sleep and appetite loss, insecurity about the future, anxiety, nightmares, speech difficulties, withdrawing, and acting up.[36]

The following comments open a window to what life is like under the cloud of deportation, in particular, the paralyzing fear, hypervigilance, and anxiety. These same feelings are painfully evident in the comments by Georgina Delgado, an undocumented student featured in Chapter 5.

Paralyzing Fear

1. Living in fear is something no one should have to experience. I know a student who wants to be a doctor. Every day she fears traveling from her house to the university because she might be rounded up. Another

student told me that her dad was deported to El Salvador when she was a kid. Immigration came to her house and just took him away.

2. One time, the *migra* came to the place of work of my boyfriend's mom and rounded up all the illegals. She wasn't there that day, so nothing happened to her. But that type of experience sears itself in one's brain and can paralyze a person.

Hypervigilance

1. I'm undocumented and live in constant fear that the *migra* (a.k.a. ICE agents) will grab me, especially now that there's so much vigilance. It's difficult to get anything done without papers. When I hear on the radio that they're rounding up illegals, I refuse to leave my home and call my parents and brothers and sisters to tell them to be careful. I was brought here when I was just a year old and if I were ever rounded up and deported to Mexico I don't know what I would do because this is my country. It's the only country I've ever known. I've never lived in Mexico and if I had to go live there I'd be lost. I just hope that one day they'll give an amnesty so that I can live without fear.[37]

2. My uncle had been in this country for five years when he was caught driving without a license and deported. His truck was confiscated and he lost his job and his few possessions in the small room he rented. He came back a year later but had to start all over again. But he doesn't drive any more and he's always afraid to go out.

3. During my first years in this country I lived in constant fear of being arrested and deported. For a young child of 7, I was really well informed about all legislative developments related to immigration. I used to sit every day in front of the TV to learn about any news that could help my family. I never told my parents how scared and anxious I was because I didn't want to add to their stress. The only place where I felt safe was at church, not even at home.

Separation Anxiety

1. Children of illegal immigrants who were born in this country have no concept of their parents' country of origin. When their parents get deported they have two options; stay in this country alone since they are citizens, or leave with their parents and adapt to a country and culture that is not their own.

2. Three years ago my sister decided to cross the border into the U.S. with her husband. I remember we were all very nervous thinking about all the dangers that awaited them. We waited and waited and then we got this call. It was my aunt calling us to tell us that they had been stopped at the border and put in jail.

3. My aunt was stopped by immigration. We were in Mexico coming back into the U.S. from vacation when they made her get out of the car and told her to go into a room. I was only 13 years old and was very frightened and didn't understand what was going on. When my aunt came out of the room, I could tell she had been crying and I could tell that something was wrong. My dad said she would not be coming back with us. I started scolding him for leaving her behind. But there was nothing he could do; her student visa had expired. He told me she would come back in a few years. But many years have passed and she has not returned.

LOOKING BEYOND THE STRUGGLES: ANTIFRAGILITY

If there is a common thread running through the comments in this chapter, it is this: though the burdens faced by Latinos are great, they are not insurmountable. Latinos have at their disposal powerful tools for rising above their hardships and achieving well-being and success. Chief among these is the family—the force of its values, strength of its members, and the wisdom of its practices.

The final story in this chapter speaks to another tool. Heretofore unexplored, but very much present in the youth cited in this book, is the notion of *antifragility*. Nassim Nicholas Taleb, an authority on this topic, describes it as follows: "Antifragility is beyond resilience or robustness. The resilient resists shock and stays the same; the antifragile gets better."[38]

The life of Yolanda Lousia Meléndrez captures the notion of antifragility. Having pulled herself out of poverty and struggled with the challenges of immigration, Meléndrez now does charity work on behalf of the less fortunate in her native Mexico. To one of the main points of this book, Meléndrez's life also speaks to the promise of U.S. Latinos, for this country, as well as others.

Someone very special was born in 1962. Her full name is Yolanda Lousia Meléndrez Gamboa, but her family and friends call her "Yoli." My mother is someone I admire very much, not just because of everything she has done for me, but also because she has a huge heart. She's always looking for ways to help the poor—humans and animals alike. That is why she's an idol to me and those who know her.

Born in Guadalajara, Mexico, she grew up in poverty. Her dream of improving her life and giving her children a future spurred her to move to the United States. At the young age of 18 she left her native country and moved to Long Beach, California to start a new life with my dad.

Although she's lived away from Mexico for a long time, she maintains a strong love of her native land and people. Whenever we visit Mexico she takes boxes full of toys, food, blankets, clothes, etc. for the poor. She loves to visit orphanages and give the children toys at Christmas time. When she returns home to California, she's always sad for the children and wishes she could bring them all to live with us.

My mom doesn't just help people. She also helps animals. I remember once when on vacation in Tijuana she saw a dog that was bleeding. She was so moved by his suffering, that she took the dog to the veterinarian who determined that a firecracker had blown up near its stomach. My mom paid for all costs and with the help of the vet was able to save the dog's life. I'll never forget the dog's face after the operation that saved his life. It's like he knew what she had done for him.

DISCUSSION QUESTIONS

1. Review Robert Rueda and Carmen DeNeve's words at the beginning of this chapter about the importance of building bridges between students' home cultures and the cultures of their schools. In light of the information presented here, what steps would you take toward this end?

2. Consider the following words by a 25-year-old Latina, cited in a study by the Pew Hispanic Center: "With us [Latinos], our grandmother lives in the house, our grandfather is there, our uncle lives with us and we can stay in the house till whenever. They [parents] don't ever ask you to move out. [They'll say] 'Until you get old enough, you're good, you help us pay some bills. You don't have to leave.' It's like 'You're living with us.'"[39] What Latino family values are exemplified in this quote? What are the positives and negatives that might arise from the situation described?

3. What are some common stereotypes surrounding the American family and American gender roles? Where do these stereotypes come from? What element of truth do they capture and where do they go wrong? What might be the source or origin of some of these stereotypes?

4. How are Latinos and Latino families depicted in movies and television shows? How do these representations compare with the realities depicted in this chapter?

5. Besides Yolanda Lousia Meléndrez, can you find other comments or stories in this and other chapters that illustrate the notion of antifragility?

RESOURCES

Avance (http://www.avance.org)
A program that provides innovative education and family support services to predominantly Latino families in low-income at-risk communities. It is dedicated to promoting school readiness and supporting family engagement.

Colorín Colorado (http://www.colorincolorado.org/families/)
A bilingual website featuring reading resources and strategies. For parents, the site provides reading tips and suggestions for partnering with teachers. For teachers, there is also information on Hispanic families and resources for working with English language learners.

The Center for Family Studies at the University of Miami (http://bsft.org)
The nation's largest clinical intervention center for Latino families and other minority groups. The center's publications and training services help train psychologists who work with Latino families.

Encuentro Latino (http://latinodv.org/)
A national resource center and technical assistance provider on domestic violence in Latino communities.

GobiernoUSA.gov (http://www.usa.gov)
A U.S. government website that provides information on a variety of topics, including those related to family life.

The Latino Family Literacy Project (http://www.latinoliteracy.com)
A website that offers training workshops for teachers and Latino parents to promote a regular family reading routine and develop strong English language skills.

LatinoFamilies.net (http://latinofamilies.wordpress.com/)
A website dedicated to helping people connect to resources that will help them better serve Latinos in their communities.

The National Alliance for Hispanic Families (http://www.hispanicfamily.org)
An organization that promotes strategies, research, and programs that strengthen Hispanic families.

The National Campaign to Prevent Teen and Unplanned Pregnancy (www.teenpregnancy.org)
A national organization dedicated to helping families and improving the well-being of children through the prevention of teen pregnancy.

The Pew Hispanic Center (http://pewhispanic.org)

A project of the Pew Research Center that publishes studies and surveys on a range of issues pertaining to U.S. Latinos, including the family.

U.S. Department for Health and Human Services Administration for Children and Families (http://www.childwelfare.gov/systemwide/cultural/fami lies/hispanic.cfm)
A government website on Latino family topics and resources.

NOTES

1. Lorena Garza González and Lisa Treviño Cummins, *Inheritance: Discovering the Richness of Latino Family and Culture*. Arlington, VA: Urban Strategies, 2012.

2. Robert Rueda and Carmen DeNeve, "How Paraeducators Build Cultural Bridges in Diverse Classrooms." *Community Circle of Caring Journal* 38, no. 2 (n.d.): 53–55.

3. Unless otherwise noted in a separate footnote, all data cited in this section come from the U.S. Census Bureau (www.census.gov).

4. "Between Two Worlds: How Young Latinos Come of Age in America." *Pew Hispanic Center,* December 11, 2009. http://pewhispanic.org/files/reports/117.pdf.

5. Ruthie Flores and Katie Sullentrop, "An Overview of National Data on Latinos." *The National Campaign to Prevent Teen and Unplanned Pregnancy,* November 15, 2007. http://www.thenationalcampaign.org/resources/pdf/FastFacts_TPChi ldbearing_Latinos.pdf.

6. Ibid.

7. Ibid.

8. Paul Tough, *How Children Succeed. Grit, Curiosity, and the Hidden Power of Character*. New York: Mariner Books, 2013.

9. Andrea Martinez, "Chivas Reserve Coach Resigns to Head for South Africa." *Goal,* June 3, 2010. http://www.goal.com/en-india/news/140/world-cup-2010/2010/06/03/1957253/manchester-united-striker-javier-Hernándezs-father-quits.

10. David Hayes-Bautista, "Challenges/Los Desafíos." In *Chicken Soup for the Latino Soul: Celebrating La Comunidad Latina,* edited by Jack Canfield, Mark Victor Hansen, and Susan Sánchez-Casal, 380. Cos Cob, CT: HCI, 2005.

11. Andrew J. Fuligni, "Family Obligation and the Academic Motivation of Adolescents from Asian and Latin American, and European Backgrounds." In *Family Obligation and Assistance during Adolescence: Contextual Variations and Developmental Implications (New Directions in Child and Adolescent Development Monograph),* edited by A.J. Fuligni, 61–76. San Francisco: Jossey-Bass, Inc., 2001.

12. Constance M. Yowell, "Possible Selves and Future Orientation: Exploring Hopes and Fears of Latino Boys and Girls." *Journal of Early Adolescence* 20 (2000): 245–80.

13. Robert Rueda and Carmen DeNeve, "How Paraeducators Build Cultural Bridges in Diverse Classrooms." *Community Circle of Caring Journal* 38, no. 2 (n.d.): 53–55.

14. Gloria Estefan, "Gloria Estefan." *iWise: Wisdom on Demand,* n.d. http://www.iwise.com/W4LkC.

15. Isabel Valdés, *Marketing to American Latinos: A Guide to the In-Culture Approach. Part I.* Ithaca, NY: Paramount Market Publishing, Inc., 2000.

16. Alberta M. Gloria and Theresa Seuar-Herrera, "Ambrosia and Omar Go to College: A Psychological Examination of Chicana/os in Higher Education." In *The Handbook of Chicana/o Psychology and Mental Health,* edited by Roberto J. Velazquez, Leticia M. Arellano, and Brian McNeill. Mahwah, NJ: Lawrence Erlbaum Associates, Inc., 2008.

17. Flores and Sullentrop, "An Overview of National Data on Latinos."

18. Ibid.

19. Sarah Elkins, "Learning to 'Think Twice': A New Salvo in the Fight to Prevent Latino Teen Pregnancy." *Newsweek Magazine,* October 30, 2007. http://www.newsweek.com/2007/10/29/learning-to-think-twice.html.

20. Stephen T. Russell, Faye C. H. Lee, and Latina/o Teen Pregnancy Prevention Group. "Practitioners' Perspectives on Effective Practices for Hispanic Teenage Pregnancy Prevention." *Perspective on Sexual and Reproductive Health* 36, no. 4 (July–August 2004): 142–49.

21. *Listening to Latinas: Barriers to School Graduation—Executive Summary.* National Women's Law Center & Mexican American Legal Defense and Educational Fund, June 9, 2009.

22. Patricia Covarrubias, *Culture, Communication and Cooperation: Interpersonal Relations and Pronominal Address in a Mexican Organization.* Roman and Littlefield, 2002.

23. Rosa María Jiménez, "Spanglish: The Language of Chicanos." *Prized Writing: The Essay and Scientific & Technical Writing* no. 1995–1996 (n.d.). http://prizedwriting.ucdavis.edu/past/1995-1996/201cspanglish201d-the-language-of-chicanos.

24. Ana Celia Zentella, *Building on Strength: Language and Literacy in Latino Families and Communities (Language and Literacy Series).* Language and Literacy Series. Teachers College Press, 2005. http://www.amazon.com/Building-Strength-Language-Literacy-Communities/dp/0807746037.

25. Angela Valenzuela, *Subtractive Schooling: U.S.-Mexican Youth and the Politics of Caring.* October 2, 1999. Albany: State University of New York Press, 1999.

26. Paul Tough, *How Children Succeed.* New York: Mariner Books, 2013.

27. Cynthia García Coll, Flannery Patton, Amy Kerivan Marks, Radosveta Dimitrova, Rui Yang, Gloria A. Suarez, and Andrea Patrico, "Understanding the Immigrant Paradox in Youth: Developmental and Contextual Consideration." In *Realizing the Potential of Immigrant Youth,* edited by Ann S. Masten, Karmela Liebkind, and Donald J. Hernández. New York: Cambridge University Press, 2012.

28. Gabriel P. Kuperminc, Natalie J. Wilkins, Cathy Roche, Anabel Alvarez-Jimenez, and T. Jaime Chahin, "Risk, Resilience, and Positive Development among Latino Youth." In *Handbook of US Latino Psychology,* edited by Gustavo Carlo, Josefina M. Grau, Margarita Azmitia, and Natash J. Cabrera. Thousand Oaks, CA: Sage Publications, 2009.

29. Marcelo Suárez Orozco and Carola Suárez Orozco, *Children of Immigration.* Cambridge, MA: Harvard University Press, 2001.

30. Kuperminc, Wilkins, Roche, Alvarez-Jimenez, and Chahin, "Risk, Resilience, and Positive Development among Latino Youth."

31. Ibid.

32. Danielle Dellorto, "Doctors Working in Fast-Food Restaurants." *CNN,* July 4, 2013. http://www.cnn.com/2013/07/04/health/latino-doctors.

33. Randy Bomer, Joel E. Dworin, Laura May, and Peggy Semingson, *Miseducating Teachers about the Poor: A Critical Analysis of Ruby Payne's Claims about Poverty.* New York: Teachers College Record, 2008.

34. Tim H. Gindling and Sara Poggio, *Family Separation and the Educational Success of Immigrant Children.* Policy Brief. Department of Public Policy, University of Maryland, Baltimore County, March 2009.

35. Andrea Smith, Richard LaLonde, and Simone Johnson, "Serial Migration and Its Implications for the Parent-Child Relationship: A Retrospective Analysis of the Experiences of the Children of Caribbean Immigrants." *Cultural Diversity and Mental Health* 10, no. 2 (May 2004): 107–22.

36. *Keeping Families Connected.* Post Deportation Human Rights Project. Boston College's Center for Human Rights & International Justice, 2008–2009.

37. Since the writing of this comment, the law has changed, such that young immigrants who meet certain qualifications of the DREAM Act are not subject to deportation.

38. Nassim Nicholas Taleb, *Antifragile: Things That Gain from Disorder.* New York: Random House, 2014.

39. "Between Two Worlds: How Young Latinos Come of Age in America."

FIVE

Family Life, Latino-American Style

This final chapter offers an in-depth look at three Latino families in the Los Angeles area. Interviewed multiple times over the course of six months, their stories offer a multifaceted look at the experience of first-generation Latinos and their children, starting with the circumstances that prompted their journey to the United States to the obstacles encountered once here to their prospects and dreams for the future.

Most, if not all, of the experiences and perspectives presented here have been discussed before. For example, the stresses of being labeled a Spanish speaker in school are examined at length in Chapters 1 and 2. What distinguishes the treatment of these and other issues in this chapter is that they are situated in the larger context of the personal history of different individuals within the family unit. This approach opens up new perspectives on the U.S. Latino experience, particularly the solutions and strategies developed by the children in response to various challenges and opportunities that come their way.

The family emerges as a powerful resource, a binding element and essential support in times of trouble, as well as an impetus for new ventures. It is also a critical unit of socialization, orienting adults as to the ways of this country and instilling values and beliefs in children that are conducive to their success, particularly respect of family and authority, a sense of obligation toward others, gratitude, deference for education, and optimism about the future.[1] The notions of *familismo*, *cariño*, *respeto*, and *educación*, discussed in Chapter 4, play a central role in the family interactions depicted here, functioning as critical resources for dealing with the many challenges discussed in this book.

Other strengths such as resilience, grit, optimism, and gratitude also play a vital role in the success of the youth and their parents. Antifragility, a concept introduced in Chapter 4, which refers to the property of deriving benefit from stressors and becoming better as a result, is also present, in particular, in María Colucci's assessment that the challenges of her childhood have made her stronger.

Despite their divergent backgrounds and immigration histories, the families featured here share strikingly similar trajectories in the United States. This is especially true as it pertains to the children, who, away from their parents, bear little trace of their past—not in their bearing or manner of speaking, and especially not in their dreams and aspirations. It is only in the context of their family life that their remarkable journeys and quiet triumphs are thrown into relief.

However, these young people are not just mere products of their past. They are also individuals with their own personalities and perspectives. Nowhere is this more evident than in their answers to questions about how to improve the schooling experience of Latino youth. The at-times opposing viewpoints of siblings serve as a reminder that one-size solutions cannot address the needs of all Latino children. For that reason, while the general plan behind efforts directed at helping these children should be grounded on principles that apply to Latinos as a whole, the implementation of all such efforts should take into consideration individual differences.

Well-adjusted, accomplished, and driven, the young people in this chapter and their families bring us full circle to our claim in Chapter 1 that Latino immigration represents an opportunity from which we can benefit, provided that we confront the obstacles that keep Latino children from achieving their potential and build on their strengths, particularly their cultural and family resources.

These Latinos also speak to the enduring qualities of the American dream that have captured the imagination of people from around the world. Their stories bring to mind Dr. Quiñones-Hinojosa's view of the American dream. Born in a small village in Mexico, "Dr. Q" arrived in the United States and worked his way up from farmworker to practicing neurosurgeon and professor at Johns Hopkins University. In his autobiography, he writes:[2]

> As I would learn later on, developed countries will always welcome the
> Einsteins of this world—those individuals whose talents are already

recognized and deemed to have value. This welcome doesn't usually extend to the poor and uneducated people seeking to enter the country. But the truth, supported by the facts of history and the richness of immigrant contribution to America's distinction in the world, is that the most entrepreneurial, innovative, motivated citizen is the one who has been given an opportunity and wants to repay the debt.

The notion of repaying a debt is very much present in the mind-set of the young people featured in this chapter, and not just a debt to their adopted country, but also their debt to their parents, who have sacrificed so much for them. Also present in their comments is the notion of paying it forward by using their skills to the benefit of future children of immigration.

Before turning to the interviews, a note about the use of names in this chapter is in order. While none of the individuals interviewed for this chapter asked that we change their name, we have chosen to do so out of concern for their privacy. All other aspects of their experience remain unaltered.

THE COLUCCI FAMILY

They bear a strong resemblance to immigrants who came to America through Ellis Island at the turn of the 20th century. Marina and daughter María are tall, blonde, and blue-eyed, while older daughter Ana (also featured in Chapter 1) and dad Andrés have swarthy Mediterranean good looks. They speak proudly of their European heritage—Marina, of her Croatian and Italian grandparents, and Andrés of his Italian great-grandparents. But they reserve their greatest praise for the traditions of their country of birth, Argentina. Though two decades have passed since the Coluccis left their homeland, they still cheer for the Argentinean national soccer team, drink mate (an infusion) in the afternoons, and celebrate special events with an "asado" (Argentinean barbecue). In this regard, they are quintessential Argentineans. But having come to this country in pursuit of liberty, prosperity, and a better life for their children, they are also quintessential Americans.

The Coluccis came to the United States in 1992. Andrés, a ship captain with an Argentinean shipping company, and Marina, a retired stewardess and teacher by training, set up home in the Los Angeles area with their two daughters, Ana, 11, and María, 9, at the time.

Not ones to leave anything to chance, Andrés and Marina carefully planned every aspect of their move. He would continue working for his longtime employer, an Argentinean shipping company, and return home to Los Angeles in between assignments. She would start a day care with a childhood friend who lived nearby. The day care, which was going to be run out of the Colucci home, would supplement Andrés's income and make it possible for Marina to be home with the girls after school.

To prepare the girls for the move, they devised a strategy that drew on the family's love of travel. As Marina explains: "We wanted something better for our daughters, but we knew that it would be difficult at first, so we told them that we were setting off on a great adventure. And we made a deal: we would all help each other get through the difficulties, but if anyone could not take it, if anyone insisted on going back, we would all go back together. Our fates were sealed together."

This plan was put to the test a few short months after their arrival, when Marina's only brother unexpectedly passed away in Argentina at the age of 42, leaving two young children behind and her aging parents alone. Further adding to her grief and threatening the family's financial stability, Marina's longtime friend and would-be partner in the day care also passed unexpectedly soon thereafter. Under the circumstances, Marina and Andrés decided that the only course of action was to cut their losses and go back to Argentina, if not for good, at least for a while.

But Ana would have none of it. Like her parents, she was one to make plans. Hers involved becoming a veterinarian, and that meant doing exceptionally well in school. She figured she needed to take summer school in the upcoming months to perfect her English so as to maximize her chances of success in the next school year. She was unwavering. She told her mom to go back to Argentina and reassured her that she could take care of herself and her little sister until their dad came back from his assignment. There was no dissuading her. In the end, Marina had no choice but to stay. Her determined young daughter had flipped the family's plan on its head: one of them wanted to stay, so they would all stay.

To make ends meet and to show that she could provide for her family—a requirement for the green card—Marina took a job delivering newspapers seven days a week from 1:00 A.M. to 7:00 A.M. Thus it went for four years. On the weekends, Ana and María went along to help out. Ana folded the papers and María carried them to their destination. Sometimes, they would run into a schoolmate. For the most part, these encounters were mildly awkward, but quickly forgotten. But Marina recalls that once or twice the mother of one of those schoolmates called the newspaper to complain about that the paper was not being left exactly where she liked it. "I felt so bad for the children." Further elaboration reveals that it's not her kids she's talking about, but the children of the demanding mother. She explains: "They seemed so embarrassed by their mom. We did our best to reassure them that it was fine and that we would try harder."

Andrés throws his head back and chuckles with delight—"See, that's Marina for you. She loves everyone, skinny people, fat people, babies, old people, nice people, mean people … everyone. Not me, I'm more selective. But she loves everyone."

If Marina is all love, Andrés is all self-effacement. It's difficult to keep him in the room during the course of the interview and even more difficult to get him to open up. As he tells it, there is nothing noteworthy about him. No lessons for anyone. Nothing worth talking about.

Marina and the girls beg to disagree.

Roughly a year after arriving in the United States, Andrés found himself out of a job, as a result of changes in the shipping industry. He took a job with a cruise line in the United States. This meant going back to school for additional training and starting over as an officer, a big step down from captain. Over the course of time, he would work his way up to Chief Officer, a noteworthy accomplishment, which he dismisses with a quick wave of his hand, even as María brags about it. He explains:

> It wasn't so hard for me. I had the maturity and the personal resources to deal with the little difficulties that presented themselves, like the humiliation of not being able to express myself as well in English as I did in Spanish. You know, when you've been a captain, it can be embarrassing to make those kinds of mistakes. But, really, this wasn't so bad. I had a job and was very experienced at it. My primary concern was for Marina and our daughters, who had to fend for themselves while I was away. I used to worry a lot about them.

The years ahead brought additional worries. The family faced serious financial hardships. Andrés developed diabetes, which effectively ended his career as a navigator and Marina suffered a debilitating back injury, as well as other health problems. And as Marina's parents grew older and their health started to fail, she worried constantly about them and yearned to be by their side. She worked extra long hours and scrimped to provide round-the-clock help for them and pay their medical bills. There were also care packages, multiple daily calls, and yearly visits to Argentina when Marina would use her vacation time to attend to her parents' affairs. Through it all, Marina remembers drawing strength from the memory of her maternal grandmother who had immigrated to Argentina at the age of 14, leaving her family behind in Croatia. "She made me strong, her courage, her determination."

Sounding a lot like her mom, María reflects on the early days of the family in the United States. "They made me strong and gave me an appreciation for what we had. I learned about the power of hard work and the importance of not taking anything for granted. They also made us closer to each other."

It's hard to find flaws with her logic. Now in their early 30s, María, a dermatologist, and Ana, a veterinarian, are thriving. Their parents speak proudly of their accomplishments—of Ana's graduation with honors from one of the most selective veterinary schools in the country (the University of California, at Davis) and of the many medical schools that aggressively recruited María (some, even offering a full scholarship). She turned down them down, opting for UC Davis, so that she could live with her sister and to be a half a day's drive away from her parents.

After finishing their studies, the young women headed back down to Southern California, to be close to their parents and each other. María explains: "We love each other. We love spending time together. We want to remain a family. And of course, it's our turn to take care of our parents. They've done so much for us."

With the challenges of the early years behind them, Marina and Andrés now run a day care together out of their home. On their front lawn sits a big plastic toy ship, a favorite of the children, and perhaps also a nod to Marina and Andrés's love of adventure and of their travels. In true Argentinean form, they greet the children and their parents every morning and send them home at the end of the day with a hug, a kiss, and a smile. They teach the children the songs and games of their home country. True to her own family traditions, Marina cooks for them every day—"real food, not canned or frozen stuff, but healthy, real, home meals. Posho (chicken) and ehpinacah (spinach)," she says in her unmistakable Argentinean accent.

Cards and pictures from former students adorn their walls and speak to the love and respect that Marina and Andrés command. They remember the name of every child and parent they've ever welcomed into their home and they keep tabs on them. Though they do not say it, it's clear that Marina and Andrés have found fulfillment and joy. With good reason: they have accomplished exactly what they set out to do: raise well-adjusted, loving, and successful "chicas" (young women).

We ask the young women about what would help other immigrant children meet with the same success. Her father's daughter, María does not want to make the conversation about her, but with some prodding she brings up an incident seared in her memory. Shortly after starting school in the United States, she was scolded for making her classmates feel uncomfortable by standing too close to them. "This was very humiliating and hurtful for me."

Andrés interrupts to restate the problem in falsetto humorously copying the principal of the school who summoned him to her office: "She is not respecting other children's space." He shakes his head and adds now in his own voice—"But she wasn't doing anything wrong, she was just behaving like an Argentinean. We stand much closer to each other and touch each other more. I used to do the same thing myself at first. Now I'm very cautious. You never know who might take offense."

Bringing the conversation back to the question of how to foster success in immigrant children, María explains: "Schools should value the home culture more and bring it into the classroom. But they don't do that. And so immigrant children have to compartmentalize their lives to blend in among other students. They end up pushing aside their home life and language while in school. It's difficult to feel confident and connect with the school when that happens. ... There is a gap between the home and the school, but there should be bridges."

She pauses. Her next comment takes the conversation in a different direction: "When you come from some other place, it's difficult to find people like you. That doesn't mean that you cannot connect with others nor have deep friendships. It just means that you live with an awareness of a gap in your life." Marina jumps in: "She needs someone who understands where she comes from, someone like herself."

Ana has found such a person: her high school sweetheart and now husband, Bob. Affectionate, hardworking, easygoing, Bob is right at home with the Coluccis. At ease among Argentineans and with a love of their culture, he would pass for an Argentine were it not for the fact that he does not speak Spanish. But as Ana explains, that will change: "Speaking Spanish in the home will be important when we have kids. We both understand that. Even though Bob doesn't speak it he certainly understands it. That will be a priority. They will learn Spanish at home. It will help them in the world when they are older and help them understand their background."

For all her love of Spanish and her heritage, Ana believes that Latino students are best served by being integrated into the mainstream curriculum alongside their non-Latino peers. Her experience with the ESL track (described in Chapter 1) mirrors that of other students cited in previous chapters.

I think one of the things that I think hurt me more than helped initially coming to the United States was ESL class. I got lumped in with all the

English-as-a-second-language speakers and essentially fell through the cracks. I was too advanced in my English that I didn't have anything to learn in ESL according to the teacher, but they had no place for me in the "regular" English class. I ended up doing self-study with no guidance for my "English period" with another two girls that also didn't fit into any class. We took care of the "secret garden" the English classes had started after reading the story with the same name. We played outside. We could have done anything we wanted without supervision. Looking back now we were too young to have a "free period" at 6th grade and we missed an organized English class and had no direction. The lack of guidance could have really hurt our grades and consequently our chance at a good school and career. The good side was that we were all individually driven and eager to advance ourselves and did in fact work at our language skills by going to the library and reading for the period, but we should have had guidance. Realizing we don't all fit into a box of "English as second language" vs. "English speaker" is important. I think having more individual counseling and guidance is important to encourage Spanish-speaking children to fit into and succeed in school. Let them have the same opportunities and help them through it to succeed without separating them from their peers. We all live in the same society after all. At least that's what I wished I had.

How can this view be reconciled with María's view that schools should recognize and build on immigrant children's home culture? María offers this by way of clarification: "What I mean is that when schools ignore the home culture or relegate it to the ESL classroom, they send the message that the home is part of the problem. Schools should bring the home culture out of the margins of the ESL classroom into the center of the school and treat it for what it is; a resource."

Judging by what the Colucci's have accomplished, it's hard to quibble with that view.

THE DELGADOS

As it was with the Coluccis, so it was with the Delgados: Political instability brought them to the United States, and a child's will kept them here. That child, Georgina, arrived in the United States at the age of 13. Eight years later, she is virtually indistinguishable from any other young American of her age. She speaks English without an accent, attends college, and has big plans for the future. But she is not like any other young American. For seven years, she lived the life of an undocumented immigrant.

This changed in June 2012, when the Obama administration announced it would no longer deport young immigrants who met certain qualifications of the DREAM Act, a legislative proposal that would grant temporary residency to minors. This development, coupled with the passage of the California DREAM Act in June 2010, which allowed undocumented college students to pay in-state tuition and apply for financial aid, unlocked three critical resources for Georgina: college, a driver's license, and a work permit.

Back in 2006, when Angie and Eduardo Delgado set off for the United States with their young daughter, the DREAM Act was not on their mind. "We just wanted to give our daughter a safe and promising future, away from the political and financial instability of Venezuela," Eduardo explains. They left it all behind in pursuit of this goal—family, a small but comfortable apartment of their own, and satisfying jobs, Angie's as a preschool teacher and Eduardo's as the owner of a small electronic repair shop.

With Eduardo's sister living in Los Angeles, this was the logical destination for the family. Eduardo's sister had come here years earlier as a college student and put roots down after marrying an Angeleno. After a short stay in her house, enough for them to get their bearings, the Delgados set out on their own, subletting a friend's studio apartment while he traveled. Georgina settled into school while Angie found a job as a nanny and Eduardo as a driver for tourists and other visitors.

Eduardo knew his way around Southern California, having spent time with his sister a few years earlier. Georgina had also been here before and loved it. However, it was different for Angie. "I pined for my family and friends in Venezuela, our cozy apartment, my job … and I found it unbearable to live with the fear of deportation." Eventually, she decided that she could no longer take it. They needed to go back. Eduardo agreed to follow Angie. Not Georgina. Sounding a lot like Ana Colucci, she explained to her parents that her future—and theirs—was here, not in Venezuela. She was going to study hard and make something of herself. She would take care of them.

The parents faced a difficult quandary. They could return home and leave Georgina here with her aunt, perhaps giving her legal guardianship. However, with the economic downturn of Venezuela and Eduardo's business liquidated long ago, going back meant that the adults would face enormous economic uncertainty, in addition to the emotional pain of being separated from their only daughter. Or they could just hang tough and stay here together, with all the sacrifices that entailed for the adults. They chose the latter option.

This was not the last time they would face such a choice. A few years later, they learned that their vacant apartment in Venezuela was about to be given to strangers as part of a government initiative to alleviate the country's housing shortage. The Delgados were all too familiar with this practice. This had happened before with a small country home that Angie and her siblings had bought for their parents in their retirement years. When the parents passed away and the house was left vacant, strangers moved in. City dwellers unprepared for the rigors of the Venezuelan countryside, the strangers eventually abandoned the house, in ruins. With no financial resources to spare, Angie and her siblings had no choice but to give up the property for good.

But giving up their apartment was not an option for the Delgados. Angie explains: "It was all we had. Eduardo and I had worked very hard to buy this apartment. We couldn't just let it go. We'd have nothing if we lost it. Where would we go if we had to go back?" It was decided that Eduardo would return to Venezuela and move into the apartment, thereby halting the appropriation proceedings. Of course, this meant that they would be separated with no certainty as to when they would be together again. "This was one of the darkest moments for us," Eduardo remembers. "Not even immigration reform, where we had been hanging our hopes, would help us now. Sure, reforms would make it possible for Angie and Georgina to stay in the US and lead normal lives, but I would have no way to come back here to be with them. But what else could we do? There was no other option."

But to their surprise, another option presented itself: a trusted relative offered to move in to the apartment. Under the climate of desperation that prevailed in Venezuela, trust was of the essence and in short supply. People were known to betray friends and relatives to secure themselves a place to live. They would move in under the guise of helping out and then stay indefinitely, effectively taking ownership of the property. But this relative had their confidence. Their apartment would be safe.

The Delgados had weathered yet another crisis. The family would stay together in the United States. With various immigration reforms under discussion in Washington, D.C., there was hope for them.

And then, Eduardo had his accident. He fell off a ladder while working as a painter and broke both of his wrists. Without the use of his hands, he could not hold down a job. Indeed, he couldn't even take care of his most basic needs at home. Angie and Georgina took turns looking after him, feeding him, dressing him, and so forth. If there was one saving grace in all of this, it was that Georgina had just recently obtained a work permit and a driver's license, which made it possible for her to pick up the slack. Even so, the family depleted its savings and faced unprecedented hardship. Remarkably, they still managed to send a little back to their relatives in Venezuela every month.

Angie flashes a smile: "This is what I am most proud of—that I have been able to help my family in Venezuela. As difficult as things have been for us at times, they have been much worse for them." Angie does not dwell on these difficulties or on the sacrifices she's made. She prefers to count her blessings. "We have been very fortunate. So many people have helped us along the way. Back in Venezuela we were told that Americans were cold and uncaring. But this is not true. Americans are warm, and generous, and caring. We couldn't be more grateful. And of course, we have each other. No amount of money can compete with having an intact family." Eduardo nods, adding:

> America is a welcoming place. I have never felt discriminated against or disrespected by Americans. In fact, the only time I have felt discriminated in this country has been from other Latinos. Like the time a Mexican-American co-worker asked me what I was doing here, why I had come to the U.S. I told him that I had come for the same reason that his ancestors had come: for a better life for my family. I told him that the only thing that separated my decision from that of his family was time. What am I doing here? The same thing his relatives did earlier. We are all the same.

Eduardo speculates that Latinos who have been here for a long time may feel threatened by the newcomers but quickly adds that this is not an insurmountable problem, noting that the person who questioned his reasons for coming to this country is now a friend and supporter. Coming back to an earlier thread of the conversation, he offers this assessment of America: "Here, there is great respect for all work, whether you're a mailman, or a painter, or whatever; there is a dignity about honest work that I like very much. I think in Venezuela we are more class conscious."

With his health on the mend, Eduardo is optimistic about the future: "I am very hopeful about immigration reform and, of course, about what lies ahead for Georgina." Soon to finish an associate degree in Behavioral Science at a local community college, she has her sights set on studying culinary arts at the Art Institute of California. She wants to be a pastry chef and eventually open a bakery, perhaps employing her mom and dad.

Reflecting on how to help children such as herself, Georgina offers this:

When I was in high school, I thought I was alone, that there was no one else like me. In my high school, there were no resources for undocumented children. And so, I kept to myself, trying to make myself invisible, afraid of being found out. I lived in fear—actually, more like anxiety—especially at night. That kind of anxiety is paralyzing. You don't want to do anything because it can all disappear when you turn the corner.

Then I got to college and discovered that there are many others like me and that there are resources for us. At my school we have counselors who can steer us in the right direction and put us in touch with people who can help, like lawyers, employers, tutors. This has made a huge difference in my life. I didn't know it at the time, but it turns out that there was high school nearby with counselors for students like me. And so my advice is to have resources and make sure that the young people know about them.

She leans forward to make this last point: "Children need to feel safe and to be part of a community. They need be connected to others."

Talk of belonging prompts several questions about Venezuela: What place does it occupy in her life? What does she remember about it? Does she miss it? Would she move back if the opportunity presented itself?

It's been almost eight years since we left Venezuela. That's a long time for someone my age. But I still love my country and feel proud to be Venezuelan. I miss my friends and family, the beautiful warm beaches—they're warm year-round, you know—and the food. My mom and I love to cook Venezuelan style, but there are some ingredients that you can't get here.

I dream about going back and visiting, but I don't think I would return to live there. After eight years, it would be difficult to adjust to life, with all the political and economic problems. My life is here and there is a part of me that is American. I want my children to learn about Venezuelan culture and to see what a beautiful country I come from. I hope I can take them there one day. I want them to carry a little of Venezuela inside them.

THE RUIZ FAMILY

They are fraternal twins, though you wouldn't know it upon first meeting them. Talkative and extroverted, Mathew is the kind of person that gets noticed when he walks into a room. Pedro, on the other hand, comes across as shy, self-effacing, and reflective. Mathew is also significantly taller and bigger than his brother, which also accounts for his bigger presence. A sophomore at the University of California, Merced, he has wanted to be a lawyer for as long as he can remember. Pedro, on the other hand, wants a career in the medical field, but is still trying to decide between premed and prenursing. He will be transferring to a four-year college, upon completing his associate degree from Santa Monica Community College in 2014.

Within a few minutes of talking to them, these differences fade into the background as the similarities between them take center stage. Their manner of speaking invokes images of Southern California boys with the kind of relaxed demeanor that comes from living near sunny beaches. With their Manhattan Beach school pedigree and refined way of speaking, it would be easy to peg them as children of privilege. A small coastal city in Los Angeles's South Bay, Manhattan Beach has some of the most expensive real estate in the nation, and its schools consistently rank among the top five in California.

But Mathew and Pedro aren't children of privilege. Born in the United States to a Mexican mother, Carolina, and a Salvadorian father, Mateo, they know the struggles of immigration firsthand. Originally from Oaxaca, Mexico, Carolina started working at age seven selling *paletas* ("popsicles") in the streets after school to help her parents. At 12, she dropped out of school and left her native Oaxaca to work in Mexico City cleaning houses full time so that she could contribute more to her family, which by then had grown to seven children. "Imagine. I was separated from my mother at age 12. I was just a kid. From there on, everything I learned about life, I learned from others."

Six years later, in 1985, she packed her belongings and headed to Los Angeles with an aunt, to join another aunt who had recently lost her husband. A young woman in her prime, she had the physical stamina to withstand the rigors of a trip that proved extremely difficult for her aunt. But her youth also made her vulnerable, especially after being separated from her aunt who was traveling with a slower-moving group. Once on American soil, Carolina was approached by a coyote who told her that her aunt had asked him to look out for her. He offered the young woman a ride to a supposedly safe place, where she could spend the night and wait for her aunt. However, no sooner did Carolina get in the car, the man tried to force himself on her.

I started to scream and kick and punch as hard as I could. But he reminded me that I had no rights here. If I made a scene I would be deported. At that moment, a police car drove by and I told the coyote that I would break a window and scream for help. I said I preferred to go back to where I came from than to have to put up with what he was about to do to me. He must have believed me because he gave up and let me go. I don't know where I got the strength to respond that way. I just did. I can't help but wonder how many other girls were victimized by him.

With this ordeal behind her, Carolina settled into life in Los Angeles cleaning homes with her aunts. One such home belonged to Alice, a lawyer and single mother. Alice took Carolina under her wing, offering her a job taking care of her young son. As a condition for the job, however, Carolina needed to attend adult school at night to learn English and to learn to read and write. Seizing the opportunity to learn English and work with Alice who had always treated her with utmost respect and kindness, Carolina willingly accepted. "I was so excited about going back to school! I had dropped out of school in fifth grade. This is was a big deal for me. That's why I remind the boys to appreciate and take full advantage of the opportunities they have to educate themselves. I didn't have those opportunities. That's why I value them so much and insist that the boys do their best at school." Years later, it was through Alice that Mathew and Pedro came to have such opportunities.

Carolina met her husband-to-be, Mateo, through his sister, who was a close friend and a coworker. Mateo and his sister had come to the United States fleeing El Salvador's bloody civil war (1979–1992), which left some 75,000 dead. Fearing for his life due to his family's involvement in politics, Mateo left behind two children, along with his ex-wife, parents, siblings, and other relatives. A trained accountant, Mateo started out doing odd jobs and eventually worked his way to sales rep for a major U.S. company, going to school at night, along the way. Like the Coluccis and the Delgados, he has always been there for his loved ones back home. And he misses them terribly. He has gone back to visit a few times, and his parents have visited them here, but he regrets that his children have not grown up around them.

Mateo's sense of duty and love of family impressed Carolina:

I liked Mateo right away. He was respectful, kind, and caring. I knew his sister well and liked the values they were raised with and the way he treated his family in El Salvador. Alice really liked him—they got along really well with her, which meant a lot because she was always looking out for me. Oh, and he was not a drinker. Coming from a home with an alcoholic father, I was not about the settle down with a drinker. I know the dangers of alcohol first hand. I talk a lot about substance abuse to Mathew and Pedro and pray to God to protect them.

Carolina has every reason to believe her prayers have been answered. From the moment Mathew and Pedro were born, it seems like they have been under an aura of protection. The boys rattle off a long list of people who have helped them along the way: parents, aunts, teachers, neighbors, schoolmates, and so on. But if they have had one guardian angel, it is Alice. "She is part of our family," Pedro explains. "She's always been there for us—not just financially. Without her, we would have found it very difficult to complete the college application process with all the deadlines and steps, since our parents couldn't help us. At each level of school, she has shown us the way forward. From the time we were old enough to go to school, she made sure we got the best education possible and dealt with whatever problems came up."

Like Ana Colucci and other children quoted in this book, Mathew and Pedro have had to contend with misguided assumptions about their language abilities. Mathew recounts how he dealt with the misconception that all bilingual children need remedial courses in English:

I remember being in ESL in 4th grade and asking myself—why am I still here? I told my teachers, I don't want this any more. My brother and I speak English very well. Put us in with regular students, where we can take regular Math, English, Social Studies. I was so persistent that they eventually listened to me. And then I told the other kids in ESL to do the same. Eventually, the school did away with the ESL class for our group of students.

In high school, the young men had to contend with another common misconception: that Latinos study Spanish because they want an easy A. Deeply bothered by this view, Mathew faked an English accent when speaking Spanish and pretended to know much less than what he actually knew. "I felt embarrassed to speak Spanish and worried that the other kids would say, well, of course you're doing well in this class. So I made my accent more White. This helped me survive."

Pedro settled on a different strategy: "I didn't really pay attention to the criticism. I took Spanish because I wanted to improve my reading and writing. I did it for my own reasons, so what others thought of me didn't really matter. I'm glad I did it because I think I will be able to put my skills to use when I become a medical professional." He is so low-key that it's easy to overlook how remarkable it is for a teenager to put his long-term goals ahead of peer pressure.

The different strategies adopted by the young men—Mathew's chameleon approach and Pedro's stance of resistance—served one and the same purpose: to help them make the most of a school environment where the large majority of students is not like them. With a student population that is overwhelmingly English monolingual (90%) and only 3.5 percent Spanish speaking, the Manhattan Beach Unified School District stands in sharp contrast with the greater Los Angeles metropolitan area, one of the most multicultural and multilingual areas in the United States, if not the world.

To fit in among their Manhattan Beach peers, both young men have cultivated their American selves. Listening to them, it's easy to understand why. "A lot of teachers think that minorities aren't as intelligent so they baby us. Of course, there are people that need help, but just because my name is Pedro they assume that I need help. Sure, there are Latinos that need help, just like there are other people that need help. I always try to explain this to people." For Mathew, it's all about being treated like an individual, not a member of a group. "People ask me how I feel as a Latino about this or that issue. But why should it matter where I come from? Why do I have to be viewed through the lens of my ethnicity? I want to be Mathew, not Mathew, the Latino."

But this doesn't mean that the young men are disconnected from their heritage. In fact, in high school, they enrolled in Spanish classes against the wishes of their dad, who said they could perfect the language at home and make better use of their time in school studying another subject matter. They also joined the "Baja Club," a cultural exchange program that enabled them to spend time in Mexico and host Mexican students in their home. Part of their work for this club involved collecting computer equipment and clothes for poor families in Mexico, as well as doing volunteer work in the country during spring break. "This expanded our horizons. We realized that there was more to Mexico and being Mexican than what we had seen in LA or what we knew from visiting our grandparents in Oaxaca," Pedro explains.

In college, they no longer need to join a club in order to connect with their heritage. UC Merced and Santa Monica College are both "majority–minority" institutions, which means that minorities make up a majority of the student population, especially Latinos. For Mathew, this context presents new challenges. Whereas in the Manhattan Beach schools he stood out for being Latino, now he stands out for not being Latino enough. "I'm an outsider again, though in a different way. The Latinos think I'm wealthy and whitewashed because I come from Manhattan Beach," Mathew observes, chuckling at the irony.[3]

With a persona that is devoid of ethnic markers, he is often called "whitewashed." "Why do people call me whitewashed? Is it because I speak English well, or because I'm educated, or because I have White friends? I am an American. I was born here, raised here, and educated here. I love this country. I don't know how other people feel about that, but I know how I feel and what I am." Barely pausing to take a breath, he offers a particularly powerful example of how teachers' fixation with ethnicity can hurt students. "When I was applying to college everyone told me to write about being Latino. But why can't I write about something else? My teachers told me that that would make me stand out. In the end, I ended up writing about being Latino because I cared more about getting into college than about expressing myself in my application. But I had other things to say."

Pedro recalls getting similar advice, but he did not feel like his brother. "For one of the essays in my college application, I needed to write about a challenge in my life. Growing up in Manhattan Beach, I was an outsider, which posed challenges. This is something I overcame so I wanted to talk about it." For the other essay, which focused on leadership, Pedro wrote about being the captain of his school's cross-country team. "My teammates picked me because they said I led by example. I showed quiet leadership."

Unlike his brother, Pedro rarely gets labeled as whitewashed. He believes that it has to do with the fact that he is more comfortable speaking Spanish and expressing his ethnicity than Mathew. His shyness is also a factor. "Being so outgoing and popular, Mathew always wanted to fit in. But I have always been kind of shy and quiet, so I'm used to not being noticed as much. I don't worry as much about not fitting in. I know who I am and am comfortable with that."

Asked about how to help Latino children succeed, Mathew offers that they are best served by being treated like everyone else. Pedro agrees but is careful to point out that this does not mean that Latinos should not get special help if they need it. "But no one should assume that we all have the same needs and wants." Sounding a lot like María Colucci, he adds: "It's a balance between acknowledging students' background and not singling them out for it or boxing them in." We ask: But how are educators to know how to strike the right balance? "Ask the students. If they don't know, help them find their way," Mathew explains.

With the conversation winding down, Mathew and Pedro's little brother runs in the room. Born when the young men were in their senior year of high school, the rambunctious three-year-old wants to join the conversation with his big brothers. He is excited about attending preschool next year. "It's Alice's idea," Carolina explains, as she sits the little boy on her lap. "She wants him to get a head start." As if any such explanation were needed.

DISCUSSION QUESTIONS

1. Consider the following quote by Alejandro Portes, a renowned sociologist and expert on immigration. Which of the three paths are the youth in this chapter following? What is the role of the family in all of this?

    The question today is to what sector of American society will a particular immigrant group assimilate? Instead of a relatively uniform "mainstream" whose mores and prejudices dictate a common path of integration, we observe today several distinct forms of adaptation. One of them replicates the time-honored portrayal of growing acculturation and parallel integration into the white middle class. A second leads straight in the opposite direction to permanent poverty and assimilation to the underclass. Still a third associates rapid economic advancement with deliberate preservation of the immigrant community's values and tight solidarity.[4]

2. A well-developed body of research indicates that Latino children who retain their ties to their home culture are more likely to succeed in school and attain overall well-being than those who do not. What in this chapter could account for these findings?

3. The youth in this chapter appear to give inconsistent advice surrounding the treatment of Spanish and the home culture in schools. On the one hand, Ana and Matthew object to being viewed through the lens of these background factors. On the other, María and Pedro recommend that special consideration be given to these factors in the school context. How can these conflicting views be reconciled in light of the information presented in Chapter 1 about linguistic and academic profiling?

4. Which Latino family values discussed in Chapter 3 are exemplified in this chapter? Which practices and points of view of Latino families presented here stand in sharpest contrast with those of American families?

5. As noted at the beginning of this chapter, our purpose in presenting whole families was to open up new perspectives on the U.S. Latino experience. What new perspectives emerge from this approach?

NOTES

1. Marcelo Suárez Orozco and Carola Suárez Orozco, *Children of Immigration.* Cambridge, MA: Harvard University Press, 2001.

2. Alfredo Quiñones-Hinojosa, *Becoming Dr. Q: My Journey from Migrant Farm Worker to Brain Surgeon.* Berkeley: University of California Press, 2011.

3. As this book goes to press, Matthew will be transferring to the University of California, at Santa Barbara to complete his junior and senior year of college. For his part, Pedro has been accepted in the nursing program at San Francisco State University.

4. Alejandro Portes, *The New Second Generation.* New York: Russell Sage, 1996.

Afterword

All of the youth in this book have beaten the odds: they all have a college degree and, by all signs, a bright future ahead. Yet not a single one can lay claim to a privileged education or a carefree childhood. Some have struggled with poverty and the trials of immigration. All too many have felt the sting of discrimination. Nearly all have experienced subtractive schooling.

How did they manage to surmount these and other formidable obstacles? This is the question we set out to explore in this book. The stories relayed here converge on a surprisingly simple answer: beating the odds does not hinge on everything going right. In many cases, one or two rights can unmake a lengthy list of wrongs. A caring teacher, a supportive home environment, a validating school experience can tip the scales in favor of success.

These stories also highlight the critical value of personal strengths (particularly those associated with resilience) in overcoming adversity. Akin to antibodies, they are Latino youths' response to the forces that threaten their well-being. The take-home message about these strengths is that they are abundantly present and ripe for the taking, both by educators and by society at large.

In an era of dwindling educational resources, this message could not be more important. Small gestures of *cariño* and *respeto* by teachers and mini-initiatives such as posting welcoming messages in Spanish in the school hallways or hosting an afterschool reading club focused on issues of interest to Latino youth can go a long way toward creating an additive school environment. Likewise, modest investments in developing students' personal strengths can yield rich returns. Such investments can be as simple as posting resilience challenges in the hallways or holding a resilience collection drive where students gather stories of resilience from friends, neighbors, and family for sharing in school.

If writing and collecting stories can have an empowering effect on students, taking them in can be a transformative experience for educators. For us, the transformation came in the way of a two-part question, which posed itself to us: what are the framing principles of the teaching enterprise, and how should they be modified in light of the experiences relayed by Latino youth?

The literature on the framing principles of teaching is extensive. In the course of reviewing it, two principles by the Carnegie Mellon Eberly Center struck us as particularly relevant to our task. They are listed in abbreviated form under 1a and 2a, followed by our thoughts on how they apply to Latino youth, under 1b and 2b:

1. Framing principle of teaching by the Carnegie Mellon Eberly Center

a. Effective teaching involves acquiring relevant knowledge about students and using that knowledge to inform our course design and classroom teaching.

When we teach, we do not just teach the content, we teach students the content. A variety of student characteristics can affect learning. For example, students' cultural and generational backgrounds influence how they see the world; disciplinary backgrounds lead students to approach problems in different ways; and students' prior knowledge (both accurate and inaccurate aspects) shapes new learning.[1]

How we see this applying to Latino youth

b. Latino students' life experiences and cultural background influence how they see the world and, equally important, how they are seen by it. The perceptions of the world, particularly those of teachers and school administrators, have a direct impact on their academic and social development.

Frequently seen as an impediment to academic achievement, bilingualism, biculturalism, and Latino family values and cultural traditions are actually among the most powerful tools for bridging the

Latino academic gap. Frequently unseen, the gamut of strengths associated with resilience are also valuable assets.

To come to know and master the use of these and other resources, educators should encourage the sharing of life histories and partner with their students to understand how to parlay their stories into positive academic outcomes.

2. Framing principle of teaching by the Carnegie Mellon Eberly Center

a. Effective teaching involves recognizing and overcoming our expert blind spots.

We are not our students! As experts, we tend to access and apply knowledge automatically and unconsciously (e.g., make connections, draw on relevant bodies of knowledge, and choose appropriate strategies) and so we often skip or combine critical steps when we teach. Students, on the other hand, don't yet have sufficient background and experience to make these leaps and can become confused, draw incorrect conclusions, or fail to develop important skills.[2]

How we see this applying to Latino youth

b. Our training predisposes us to view Latino students through the lens of the research literature. This leads us to think of them primarily as members of a category of learners, to the neglect of their personal histories and individual characteristics.

The following comment by Matthew Ruiz (reproduced from Chapter 5) opened our eyes to this blind spot:

People ask me how I feel as a Latino about this or that issue. But why should it matter where I come from? Why do I have to be viewed through the lens of my ethnicity? I want to be Mathew, not Mathew, the Latino.

Matthew's comment brings to mind one of 46 "White privileges" identified by Peggy McIntosh in a seminal 1988 paper. Privilege number 21 reads as follows: "I am never made to speak for all the people of my racial group."[3]

McIntosh argues that to bring about change, we first need to identify the "colossal unseen dimensions" of these privileges. Alerting us to the dangers of seeing past the individual, Matthew's words render one such dimension visible. Like all youth, Latinos want and need to be recognized as individuals. While the research literature should inform all work and interactions with Latino youth, it should never substitute for connecting with students at a personal level. Thus, as we have come to appreciate during the course of working on this book, teaching Latinos requires balancing two competing goals at once, namely, attending to issues associated with group membership (including special needs, background factors, cultural resources, and so on) and responding to students as individuals, with unique personalities and life histories.

These are the principles that spoke to us. In short, by lifting our gaze beyond the negatives associated with Latino youth we discovered a wealth of resources seldom appreciated by educators and society at large, in particular, bilingualism and biculturalism, family and cultural values, and resilience. By reaching beyond the research literature and connecting with Latino youth at a personal level, we were reminded of the centrality of relating to students as individuals, with unique personalities and life histories. Other principles and truths are bound to assert themselves to those who consider the stories in this book and all who lean forward to listen the voices of Latino youth.

It all starts with a story. . . .

NOTES

1. Principles of Teaching. *Carnegie Mello Eberly Center. Teaching Excellence & Educational Innovation.* (n.d.) http://www.cmu.edu/teaching/principles/teaching .html.

2. Principles of Teaching. *Carnegie Mello Eberly Center. Teaching Excellence & Educational Innovation.* (n.d.) http://www.cmu.edu/teaching/principles/teaching .html.

3. Peggy McIntosh. "White Privilege and Male Privilege: A Personal Account of Coming to See Correspondences through Work in Women's Studies." 1988. Accessed May 2, 2014. http://files.eric.ed.gov/fulltext/ED335262.pdf

Index

Academic profiling, 14–16; special education courses, in, 16; subtractive schooling and, 15–16

Academic programs: Advancement Via Individual Determination (AVID), 8, 28; California Mini Corps, 29; Puente Project, 34; Summer Bridge, 27, 28

Acculturation: feelings associated with, 95; issues of sexuality and, 98–99; stages of, 96–97; value of, 93; versus assimilation, 93

Achievement gap, 5, 176–77

Adaptive distancing, strategy of, 104

Additive schooling: ingredients of, 25–30

Advancement Via Individual Determination (AVID), 8, 10, 28, 34

African American: English (Ebonics), 61; students, 3, 16

African heritage in Latin America, 84, 86

Agency: Latino youth and sense of, 68, 105–6, 137, 143

Alingual, sense of being, 58. See Falling in-between languages

Alliance for Excellent Education, 4, 33

Antifragility, 148–49, 156

Anzaldúa, Gloria, 61, 63, 80

Asian Latinos, 84–85

Avance, 150

AVID. See Advancement Via Individual Determination

Balseros, 83. See also Cubans

Bilingualism: advantages of, 67; burdens of, 51–67; circumstantial, 59; elective, 59; myth of equal and native-like abilities in two languages, 59–60; subtractive, 50; value for individuals and society, 67–68

Borderlands: properties of, 80–101; Spanish, historical use of the term, 45

Bracero Program, 45, 83, 113

Burro Genius (Villaseñor), 26

California Dropout Research Project, 33

Camacho, Analiese, 80

Cariño, 124–26; and other family
  values, 119
Carnegie Mellon Eberly Center, 176
Celebrations and traditions, 106–9;
  Christmas, 107–8; Cinco de
  Mayo, 109; *Día de los Muertos,*
  108; Dominican Day Parade,
  109; Latino Heritage Month, 108;
  Puerto Rican Day Parade, 109;
  Quinceañera, 108
Center for Applied Linguistics
  (CAL), 73
Center for Latino Family Studies, 150
Center for Multilingual and Multicul-
  tural Research, 73
Central Americans: immigration to
  the U.S., 45, 83
Character strengths that correlate
  with life satisfaction, 119, 144
Chavira, Reuben, 119
Chicano: meaning of term, 86; stud-
  ies, 16, 31
Chicano Civil Rights Movement, 86
Chicanos: Paz, Octavio on, 88;
  Spanglish and, 62
Chinese laborers in Cuba and Peru, 84
Christmas holidays in Latino culture,
  107
Cinco de Mayo, 109
Civic participation by Latinos, 82
Code-switching, 61–62
Colorín Colorado, 150
Colucci, Ana, 5–8
Colucci family, 157–62
Critical consciousness, strategy of,
  104
Cuba: annexation during Spanish-
  American War, 45; Barrio Chino,
  84; Chinese laborers in, 84
Cuban Revolution, 45
Cubans: *Balseros,* 83; immigration to
  the U.S., 45, 83; *Marielitos,* 83,
  113

Cultural stereotypes: negative consequences of, 17
Culture, 79–115; instrumental versus
  expressive, 93

Dame Edna's comments about Spanish, 39
Delgado family, 162–66
Deportation: anxiety over, 147–48;
  fear of, 146–47; hypervigilance,
  147; life under the threat of,
  146–48
Día de los Muertos, 108
Día de los Reyes Magos (Three Kings
  Day), 107
Diccionario de la Lengua Española,
  73
Discrimination: Latino-on-Latino,
  87; negative effects of, 99–101; in
  the school context, 3; in Spanish-
  speaking countries, 87; survey of
  children on, 100
Dominicans: immigration to the U.S.,
  45; U.S. demographics, 83
Dream Act, the, 153, 163
Dr. Q. *See* Quiñones-Hinojosa,
  Alfredo, Dr.

Echevarría González, Roberto, 63.
  See also Spanglish
Educación, 133–35; and other family
  values, 119
Educational attainment: Latino dropout rates, 3; Latino graduation rates,
  4; teenage pregnancy and, 129
El Instituto Cervantes, 73
Encuentro Latino, 150
English: academic, 11, 31; Latinos
  who speak it, 47; official language
  laws, 47
English as a second language (ESL)
  track: academic structure of,
  10–14; linguistic profiling and,

9–14; placement in, 9–10; subtractive schooling and, 13–14
ERIC, 34
ESL. *See* English as a second Language
Este cuerpo (Camacho), 80
Ethnic identity, 82; data on, 80; loss of Spanish and, 54; as a pathway to well-being, 101–3; properties of, 112; Spanglish and, 62–63
European immigration to the U.S., 83
Excelencia in Education (Program), 34

Falling in-between languages, burden of, 58–61
Familismo, 122–24
Family, 117–53; core values of, 119–35; impact of immigration on, 136–46; statistics about, 118; treatment of and attitudes toward sexuality, 129
Fernando of Aragón (King), 42
Framing principles of teaching, 176–77
Fuentes, Carlos, on diversity of the Spanish-speaking World, 79

Gandara, Patricia, 3, 25
Gangs, youth contending with, 23, 119
Garcia, Eugene, 4, 30, 45
Gates Millennium Scholars, 34
Gender roles, 98, 127, 129. See also *Machismo*; *Marianismo*; and *Hembrismo*
Gender stereotypes, 131–32
Ghetto language, Spanish as a, 47
GobiernoUSA.gov, 150
González, Carla, 71
Grit, 119, 156

Hembrismo, 127–29
Henry Kissinger Effect and foreign accents, 61
Hispanic: history of the term, 80; versus Latino, 86
Hispanic Association of Colleges and Universities, 112
Hispanic paradox, 136
Household statistics, 118
Hyphenated self-identification labels, 89

Identification labels used by Latinos, 85–90
Immigration: challenges for children and families, 136–48; family separation and, 145–46; history of Latino, 82–84; loss of social status and, 141–43; reversal of parent-child roles in, 136–40; stresses associated with, 136
Indigenous: languages of Latin America, 44; populations in Latin America, 84
Isabella of Castile (Queen), 42

Jefferson, Thomas, 45
Jiménez, Rosa Maria, 62, 132

Labor force, Latinos in, 1–2
Language brokering, 140–41. *See also* Translating
Language dominance and immigration to the U.S., 48–49
Las Posadas, 107
Latin America's Professional Network, 112
Latino: history and criticism of the term, 86
LatinoFamilies.net, 150
Latino Family Literacy Project, 150
Latino Heritage Month, 108

Latinos: demographics, history and settlement patterns, 83. *See also* Hispanic
League of Latin American Citizens (LULAC), 113
Linguistic hallucination, 16
Linguistic isolation, 22–25
Linguistic profiling, 9–14
Lippi Green, Rosina, 41
Loss of Spanish among Latinos: consequences of, 49–50, 54–56; pattern of, 49

Machismo, 126–27
Majority-minority institution, definition of, 170
"Mama" (Chavira), 119–22
Marianismo, 127–29. See also *Hembrismo*
Marielitos, 83
McIntosh, Peggy, 177
Menéndez, Alicia, 110
Mestizo and mestizaje: Anzaldúa, Gloria, 63; definition of, 61; linguistic, 61
Mexican-American Legal Defense and Educational Fund (MALDEF), 113
Mexican-American War, 45
Mexican Independence Day, 109, 115
Moraga, Cherie, 86
"My Latin Gift" (González), 71

Names, 90–93; naming practices in the Spanish-speaking world, 90–92; naming practices of U.S. Latinos, 92–93
National Alliance for Hispanic Families, 150
National Campaign to Prevent Teen and Unplanned Pregnancy, 150
National Center for Education Statistics, 34
National Council of La Raza, 113

National Heritage Language Resource Center (NHLRC), 73
National Hispanic Heritage Month. *See* Latino Heritage Month
Nobel Prizes in Spanish literature, 39, 73
Nonstandard language: definition of the term, 76; linguistic hallucination and, 16; U.S. Latinos and, 61, 76

Paraeducators, Latinos, 126
Paz, Octavio, 88
Pew Center, 150
Pocho, 56, 88. *See also* Paz, Octavio
Ponce de León, Juan, 45
Portes, Alejandro, 172
Poverty: 143–45; children dealing with, 144–45; impact on academic outcomes, 22–24; Latino statistics, 2, 118; lifelong consequences of, 143; segregation and, 24
Pregnancy: prevention programs, 131; teenage rates, 129
Proposition 227 and Bilingual Education in California, 22
Puente Program, 34
Puerto Ricans, 83
Puerto Rico, 83; annexation to the U.S., 45

Quinceañera, 108
Quiñones-Hinojosa, Alfredo, Dr., 156

Race, relationship between socioeconomic class and, 87–88
Recovering Spanish, difficulties associated with, 50
Religion: Latino demographics on, 82; traditions and festivities rooted in, 106–7; value to children, 106
Religious names, use of, 91
Resilience, 103–4; investing in, 175–78; strategies of, 103–6; versus antifragility, 148

Resources: on culture, 112–13; on
    education, 33–34; on families,
    150–51; on language, 73–74
Respeto, 132–33
Reversal of parent-child roles,
    138–41
Rodríguez, Richard, 112
Romance languages, 42
Ruiz, Matthew and principles of
    teaching, 177–78
Ruiz family, 166–72
Rumbaut, Ruben, 112

Saint Augustine, Florida, 45
Sánchez, Isbelda, 8–9
Schooling of Latino children, 1–37;
    climate of neglect, insensitivity,
    and hostility, 16–19; in impov-
    erished neighborhoods, 22–24;
    Latino demographics on, 9
Sense of purpose and resilience, 103
Separation anxiety, impact of, 147–48
Settlement patterns of Latinos, 83–84
Sexuality, 98–99; in Latino families,
    129–31. *See also* Gender roles;
    Pregnancy
Spain: 42; languages spoken in, 44
Spanglish: criticism, of, 61, 63;
    importance of, 62–64; writings in,
    71, 80
Spanish: AP and honor classes,
    21; burdens of speaking, 51–67;
    countries where spoken, 42–44;
    history of in the U.S., 45–46; loss
    by generation in the U.S., 48–49;
    prejudices against, 39–40; speakers
    in the U.S., 42; treatment in U.S.
    schools, 20–22; as a world lan-
    guage, 41–42
Spanish-American War, 45
Spotlight on Educational Excellence, 34
Stavans, Ilan, 40
Stereotyping and discrimination of
    Latinos, 99–101

Suárez-Orozco, Carola and Marcelo:
    model of culture by, 93–94;
    reversal of map of experience,
    136
Subtractive bilingualism, 50
Subtractive schooling: academic
    profiling and, 14–16; definition
    of, 5; the ESL track and, 13–14;
    poverty and, 22–25; Spanish and,
    20–22
Summer Bridge Program, 27–28, 34

Taleb, Nassim Nicholas, 148. *See
    also* Antifragility
Temporary Protected Status, 83
Testing in the ESL track, 53
Three Kings Day. See *Día de los
    Reyes Magos*
Tomás Rivera Policy Institute, 73
Translating: burdens of, 64–66; value
    of, 68–70. *See also* Language
    brokering

U.S. Department for Health and
    Human Services Administration for
    Children and Families, 151
U.S. Department of Education, 34
U.S. Work force: Latinos in, 1–2

Valdés, Guadalupe, 59. *See also*
    Bilingualism: myth of equal and
    native-like abilities in two lan-
    guages
Valenzuela, Angela, 5, 133
Villaseñor, Victor, 26
Virgin of Guadalupe, Feast of, 92

White: privilege, 177; use of the term
    by Latinos, 87
The White House Initiative on Edu-
    cational Excellence for Hispanic
    Americans, 34

Zentella, Ana Celia, 133

About the Authors

Maria M. Carreira is a professor of Spanish Linguistics at California State University, Long Beach in Long Beach, California, with 20 years of teaching experience and codirector of the National Heritage Language Resource Center at UCLA. She is a coauthor of four Spanish textbooks, *Nexos* (Houghton Mifflin, 2008, 2010), *Sí Se Puede* (Houghton Mifflin, 2008), *Alianzas* (Cengage, 2011), and *Cuadros* (Cengage, 2012). She has published extensively in the field of Spanish in the United States, heritage language teaching, and educational linguistics. She has a PhD in Linguistics from the University of Illinois, Urbana-Champaign.

Tom Beeman is a high school Spanish teacher with California Virtual Academies as well as a former Associate Dean for the College of Education with Irvine University in Cerritos, California. He has taught Spanish in public and private high schools as well as Spanish and linguistics at the postsecondary level. Mr. Beeman specializes in language acquisition and is currently researching issues on heritage language learners and linguistic prejudice. He holds a BA in Spanish from California State University, Long Beach, MA in Linguistics from California State University, Fullerton, as well a California Single Subject Teaching Credential in Spanish with No Child Left Behind certification.